Black Cinema Treasures

G. WILLIAM JONES

BLACK CINEMA TREASURES

LOST AND FOUND

Foreword by Ossie Davis

University of North Texas Press, Denton

Publication of this book was made possible by generous grants from The L. J. and Mary C. Skaggs Foundation and the Lee and Albert H. Halff Fund of Communities Foundation of Texas.

First Edition 1991

Requests for permission to reproduce material from this work should be sent to:
Permissions
University of North Texas Press
Post Office Box 13856
Denton, Texas 76203

The paper in this book meets the minimum requirements of the American National Standard for Permanence of Paper for Printed Library Materials, z39.48-1984.

Library of Congress Cataloging-in-Publication Data

Jones, G. William (George William), 1931–
Black cinema treasures : lost and found / by G. William Jones ; foreword by Ossie Davis. — 1st ed.
p.   cm.
Includes bibliography, filmography and index.
ISBN 0-929398-26-2 (alk. paper) : $29.95
1. Afro-Americans in motion pictures.   2. Afro-Americans in motion pictures–Catalogs.   3. Southern Methodist University. Southwest Film/Video Archives–Catalogs.   4. Tyler, Texas, Black Film Collection–Catalogs.   5. Afro-Americans in the motion picture industry–United States.   I. Title.
PN1995.9.N4J66   1991
791.43'089'96073–dc20   91-10882
                                                         CIP

Contents

791.43089
Jon

Foreword
by Ossie Davis

Ossie Davis is one of America's most outstanding and accomplished dramatic artists. He has acted, written, produced, and directed for stage, screen, and theater, winning many awards and the world's acclaim in the process.

One of the great entertainment and communications phenomenon of the last several years was an event that took place on ABC, a presentation called "Roots."

The amazing thing about "Roots" was not the content of the program, or the stories, or the good acting, but the tremendous, surprising response of the American people to this glimpse of the black experience.

A lot of us wondered why, and one of the answers that we thought might make sense was that America, by and large, is extremely hungry for some of the truth of the black experience. We know too well the mythical side of the story about black folks—we have seen it in film and on television in stereotypical presentations. But, somehow, the nation as a whole knew that there was something missing from all these presentations.

So, when "Roots" came along (which, by the way, was not nearly the best representation of the black experience possible), it was good. The American public needed to know, wanted to know, and looked in to see. Now, we have an even more authentic representation of the black experience—produced and directed, acted and scripted by black people themselves, for a black audience. This gives us a chance to satisfy even further that great need among us Americans to know all we can about each other.

Ossie Davis

The Necessity of Historical Knowledge

This film collection has many values. For me, the most important thing about this collection is my awareness that we are at a time in our history when the difference between what we were in the past, what we are now, and what we will be in the future is a matter of grave concern— not only for historians, but also for parents, for all Americans.

Our children do not know our past. History is no longer a topic that excites their interest. Every year, we have cause to comment that our children don't even know who Martin Luther King was. They never even heard of Malcom X.

"Paul Robeson? Who was that?" they may say.

And we feel sad to think that so much of the rich heritage of one particular group is being denied to the children who could profit most by being exposed to it. Now, along comes this collection which enables us to see very clearly some of the truth of what life was like for that particular group in the thirties and forties. We will now have something to show to ourselves and to our children which documents and articulates the truth of the experience that we underwent before the sixties and seventies, when everything took a tremendous change for the better.

But a lot of the young people whom I meet—young black people and young white people—know absolutely nothing of what it was like before the change came. They know about Dr. Martin Luther King, perhaps, because every year they will see the picture of him on television saying, "I have a dream!" That's a part of the current consciousness of the times. But they will not necessarily know about Malcom X, about Whitney Young, about Roy Wilkins, and about the other people who were involved in that marvelous activity.

A sort of discontinuity has taken place in the historical progress of our country. Our young people, white and black, know very little about history, care even less, and are not being taught what the past was all about. There is a historical compendium of what the past was like, ready and available for them, in motion pictures and television. It is documented for them.

"There was a past, and this is how it looked," we can say to them.

But if our black youngsters feel any interest in going back beyond the present time (because they begin to suspect that black history did not begin with Martin Luther King's speech in 1963), and they go to most of the motion pictures and television to find out what life was like for black people in older times, what they would find would be scrimpy and severely distorted. They would find Stepin Fetchit, but not surrounded by friendly blacks and a plot that makes his stupidity eloquent in another way. They would find Louise Beavers and Bill "Bojangles" Robinson; but they would also find black people depicted on the screen who used their lives, their strengths, their intelligence, their wit, and their wisdom in support of white people. This was the sort of thing that Hollywood was offering to whites and to blacks—black folks as servants, black folks as helpers, black folks whose fundamental purpose in life was to make another group comfortable, another group wealthy—to make another group serve out its historical purpose on this continent.

But now, my children—if they are interested, and if they want to find out what life was like before Martin Luther King came, what life was like when Mama and Daddy were boys and girls—they can go to this collection and see the elements of black life back then. They can see things about which they can be proud, about which they can be ashamed, about which they can be embarrassed, and things about which they can feel belongingness. All of these things are available to a larger degree now because we have found this collection of films.

The Need for Black Filmmakers: Then and Now

Here are works that were produced by independent producers who—no matter who said "no" to them—did not take "no" for an answer. They went out, they wrote the scripts, they raised the money, they produced the films, they put them in their cars and went all across the country distributing them, and they proved that there was a marketplace for such films.

For our young people to know that is absolutely indispensable. You will find, in the universities as you go about the country, film departments, art departments, and theater departments. But, in many instances, although the universities may have a significant complement of black youngsters, you will seldom find those black youngsters as a group working in those courses which teach what goes on behind the camera. And you may ask yourself "Why? Is it because the black youngster is intellectually incapable of doing anything except being in front of the camera, singing and dancing and playing ball, and things like that?"

Obviously, that is stupidity.

Then what keeps our youngsters from being interested in acquiring that knowledge? What keeps them from being interested is, of course, their supposition that there's no place in the industry for blacks who possess those skills, so why the heck should they go out and acquire that knowledge?

So a whole world of possibility is being overlooked by black youngsters whose gifts might make them outstanding exemplars, if they but take the time to learn the crafts and the skills.

My hope is that, seeing these films, knowing that this kind of work was done, knowing that this kind of filmmaking exists, will whet the appetite of those youngsters who do not now truly believe that they can make it.

Education for Winning

The whole process of education has one objective, as far as I am concerned, and that is to convert losers into winners. For black people, that means providing a different image of our possibilities in American society. If our children are not told, if they are not inspired, if they cannot really believe that there is a chance for them—no matter who they are—to make it, to acquire those skills, then they will approach the whole process of education in a negative frame of mind, almost determined not to learn, asking themselves "what the hell is the use?"

These films and the preservation and presentation of them will help those of us who want to open those minds, to spread those wings, to excite and incite those imaginations, to set fire to those dreamers. These films will be invaluable aids in that process.

The Authenticity – and Awkwardness – of These Films

Film never gave us the opportunity to define ourselves as well as we were able to do in music, in dance, and even in literature. You will find that there will be a lot of awkwardnesses in these films, because we were still trying to walk with incredible burdens on our backs. What will be seen is not, in the artistic sense, the masterpieces that we would expect. What these films indicate, however, is the potential—the knowledge that, given the chance, masterpieces would surely come forth.

The thing that interests me most about these films is not what you will see on the screen—the examples of expertise manifested in all the categories of filmmaking—so much as the fact that most of these films were made by black producers, black directors, black writers. There were black people behind the scenes, telling our black story to us as we sat in black theaters. We listened blackly, and a beautiful thing happened to us as we saw ourselves up on the screen. We knew that sometimes it was awkward, that sometimes the films behaved differently than the ones we saw in the white theater. It didn't matter. It was ours, and even the mistakes were ours, and the fools were ours, and the villains were ours, and the people who won were ours, and the losers were ours.

We were comforted by that knowledge as we sat in the dark, knowing that there was something about us up there on that screen, controlled by us, created by us—our own image, as we saw ourselves.

I was reminded, when I saw that footage from *Murder in Harlem*, where the brother went downstairs and found the body of the woman lying there, of how it would have looked in the white theaters of the time. If a black man found a body, he went into all kinds of conniptions, the brother got epileptic, and total fear of the dead possessed the brother. In some cases, as in the Charlie Chan films, the brother turned white—that's an extreme reaction!

When we wanted the reality of how black people truly reacted to death, we came to our own theater and there we were able to get the truth of our own experience.

Once again, the important thing about this collection, from my personal point of view, is that it provides documentation of a truth and the facts of our existences before the sixties and seventies.

Now, I know black folks who are embarrassed by things they see on

"The Jeffersons." We are embarrassed by things which tend to cast derogatory implications on the total group. We in the black community in America have often had to depend upon the kindness of strangers for more than we wanted to. We were at risk in more ways than other groups, and therefore, all the information about us was of tremendous import.

We knew what the meaning of the stereotypes was. We were the only group that, for a long time, was not allowed to represent itself on the stage. In the early days, blacks were represented on the stage by whites who put black on their faces. Actors of great note did that. We were the only ones who had to go through that, and we knew that the stereotypes which we saw and became familiar with were often derogatory. At best, if they were "noble," their nobility was always in the service of somebody up there, somebody white, who was the master. Hattie McDaniel, in *Gone With the Wind*, is a classic and marvelous example of a beautiful actress doing a beautiful job, but it was Hattie McDaniel as she related to the needs of Scarlett O'Hara's family. Nobody ever found out whether Hattie McDaniel in the film had any children of her own, and what she did with them while she was serving the whites. We wanted to know that side of it, too.

Some of us will find embarrassment in some of these films, but that shouldn't surprise us at all. If we had had perfect representation, then why would we have needed the sixties and the seventies? Why change, if we were having such a glorious time? No, there is much in these films which should make us uncomfortable. But they should also remind us that we are still in the process of completing those changes which were started subsequent to the making of these films.

I remember seeing these films when they were originally sent around the country. I'm old enough to remember that. Even then, there was a tremendous pride in what was up there on the screen, that those were our heroes with whom we could relate in ways that nobody else could. Identity is so essential to basic, healthy personality, and these films helped to explain to me—as a youngster in the thirties and forties— exactly who I was. There were limitations, of course, but there were possibilites also. Without them, I don't think that I would be who I am—whatever that is.

The men who made these films were in the black community and were that part of the community who were brave enough to dare to think that they could make a good living without being doctors or teachers or undertakers. They were great risk-takers, they were authors, they were con-men, they were hustlers. But always, they were magicians, storytellers, the people you always wanted to come back again even if it did cost you a little out of your pocket that you hadn't anticipated. That meant a great deal to us. They were our own, and we appreciated them as such.

There were "stars" in these films, too—names anyone would know. Paul Robeson got his start in films by Oscar Micheaux, who is one of the premiere black filmmakers. My wife, Ruby Dee, worked in some of these films. And then, there were people whose names you possibly wouldn't know: Lawrence Criner and Clarence Muse worked in these films, too. They came because they appreciated the importance of independent, self-controlled black communication, at whatever level.

The black community had a general awareness of these films. As a matter of fact, in many instances there were debates as to the value of the films. At that time in particular, the black community was very sensitive about the images that were being presented for general consumption to the public. In some of these films, those of us who had middle-class backgrounds and college educations found things that we might be very sensitive about. We knew them to be true, but we didn't want anybody else to know that they were true. We felt that somebody else would make judgments about us on the basis of these films. That was a legitimate consideration.

Still and all, even the most articulate spokesman who pointed out the "negative virtue" of these films would be found, in the dark of the theater, on the back row looking too. So, they meant a great deal to us as points of reference, even if we said we only went to see them in order to understand what we needed to do to improve our image.

A Continuing Need for Black Self-Expression in Film

In these films, you will find humor, heartbreak, funnyness, awkwardness, embarrassment, and you will find a nobility of aspiration not necessarily matched by the capacity to execute. But in it all, you will find in the films and in the circumstances in which they were produced a tremendous tribute to the human spirit. Here, we have black producers and directors creating a sub-industry to service the needs of the community whose needs were not being met by Hollywood. How did they do it? How were they able to manage? Where did they get the money? What was their objective? How did they master the intricacies of production, distribution, and exhibition? Here is a lesson of importance to young filmmakers coming along in this country, and I don't refer only to young black filmmakers.

There was an article about the tremendous amount of money being made in Hollywood and how—in spite of that—several of the studios were in serious trouble because they themselves did not make *Beverly Hills Cop*, or one of the other films that became box office hits. If the major studios have not themselves mastered the intricacies of production and distribution, and if things are so shaky even for these institutions, what must it be like for the independent filmmakers who do not have at their disposal the enormous infusion of capital and expertise and know-how the studios do?

We might find, if we look back at the phenomenon of the black filmmaking industry from the twenties through the forties, some way, some method, some knowledge which would help our independent filmmakers, upon whom we have to depend for so much. If those people, under those circumstances, could produce those works, then they must have known something we need to relearn.

We are in the midst of a communication revolution. In my younger day and age, it was necessary to study history written in books. Books were the definitive ways by which we validated the human experience. You had to have it in writing before it was real. If you didn't appear in the history books, then you were not truly human beings. Written documentation was the *sine qua non* of being anything at all which had worth and value.

More and more, that is true less and less. Validation today depends not so much on showing up in the written text as in being present in some of the plastic forms of the media—in motion pictures or on television. It is what we see that defines our values. And we as blacks, we as women, we as people who are left out, have to insist that the validation process include us now. We have to insist that our forms show up there on the screens, with all our glory, with all our marvelous human attributes, with all our scars, with the truth of who we are. Therefore, when we resurrect these films now, they have a greater meaning to the viewers than they had at the time when they were made, because back in those days the final word was the printed word. This is not necessarily true any more.

For good or ill, we validate our experiences and our values as human beings now by cameras that either put them on film or on tape. That change is taking place and we are relating to that change—we are living a lifestyle which is almost dictated by that change.

I think it was Andy Warhol who made us all feel better by saying that everybody will be a celebrity for fifteen minutes on television—and to some degree, it is true. It is happening that way. The film representation, the tape representation—that is where you go now to find out who you are. Not to the books.

We gave the world jazz, we gave the world spirituals, we gave the world dance interpretations by which America is known and famous the world over. And, given the opportunity, we can be as expressive with the camera in our hands as Louis Armstrong was with the trumpet in his hands.

Hollywood is about another matter altogether. It is not established to give ethnic and sexual minorities a chance to express who we are. That is not what Hollywood is. And as long as Hollywood isn't about that, we need some other venue, some way that groups who have a cultural statement to make can make it on film, can make it on video. We still need independent, black film expression—desperately.

The Decline of Black Filmmaking in the Fifties

The sixties and seventies provided a change, a watershed in the American experience. When the laws and customs of segregation—those rules which barred us out and made it necessary for us to produce our own films in the first place—were dismantled, we were able to go into any theater, any restaurant, to become students at any universities that we might want. This was a great triumph, a beautiful thing, a great tribute to America's flexibility. It was also proof that Dr. King's dream is capable of being realized. America has that much soul and flexibility, and we are still in the process—we haven't gotten there yet, by any means, but we know we are on our way.

But to some degree, the advances made in every aspect of black life as a result of integration also have negative connotations. For instance, the opening of the doors to blacks by all of the American educational institutions meant that good black teachers from black colleges, and the good black students, might—in many instances—leave those black colleges, which had served us so beautifully. Some of those colleges are now on the ropes, they are almost gone.

The one positive element that is beyond reproach in these films is that they represented the capacity of blacks not only to act in front of the camera, but also to take care of the myriad things that take place behind the camera. The power that operates, the decisions that are made, the managerial expertise that is called forth—the things that make the true differences in America—were being practiced by black people. Now that the black filmmaking industry of those times no longer exists, we don't have the training capacity to make available to our young folks. I produced and directed five feature films, but there was no place in Hollywood's stream of continuity for me to come in and say, "We want you to come in and be one of our growing young directors." When the fad for black films was over, the door that opened so widely for us to come in was opened twice as wide for us to go out. So long as that is one of the patterns by which the American film industry deals, we need—if only in self-defense—to have our own industry. We need to encourage independent film production. Hollywood needs innovation and new ideas, now more than ever. If Hollywood were wise and smart, they would run to establish or to support training institutions, national theaters, drama departments on the various campuses, and they would have a tax credit for supporting those institutions. Then, they would have at their beck and call all of this magnificent talent that would come from these institutions. They don't see that yet.

The major thing that I think has been accomplished by finding and restoring these films—and I reiterate this because of its importance—is that the disjuncture between us and our history, which is so important to our young folks is, in this instance, lessened because we have documentation of a very rich period in our history. We would all have been the poorer had it disappeared.

Introduction
King Tut's Warehouse: Finding the Films

In August of 1983, the offices of the Southwest Film/Video Archives at Southern Methodist University in Dallas received a call from Mr. Roy Larsen, who managed several warehouses for the Roosth and Genecov Corporation in Tyler, Texas.

"Would your Archives be interested in taking a look at what appear to be some old films which have been sitting in one of our warehouses for a long time? Nobody here wants them, they're taking up a lot of space, and we're getting ready to dispose of them unless you want them."

As Director of the Archives, my principle of collection has always been the same as that of the late Henri Langlois of the Cinematheque Francais in Paris: "If it's on celluloid, we want it." So I said I would come to Tyler, a city some 85 miles east of Dallas, as soon as I could.

That weekend in their warehouse, I saw a stack of octagonal steel film cans ten feet high, ten feet deep and ten feet wide sitting in a corner. It was obvious that these were films indeed, of the 35-millimeter size which are shown in theaters. My heart sank when I opened the first can I could get to, because a yellow-brown cloud of nitrate dust billowed out at me, signifying that at least some of these films were on pre-1950 nitrate stock, and were already in a state of decomposition. Mr. Larsen helped me pull a few more cans down off the stack. Opening them, I saw that, so far, all of the films were on the old nitrate stock, but some of them seemed to be still in good shape. What began to excite me, however, was a few of the titles which I recognized: *Murder in Harlem*, *Blood of Jesus* and *Souls of Sin*. If the films were actually what their reel-wrappers said they were, these were perhaps the last—

or the best—remaining prints of a little-known but important group of films made from the twenties through the early fifties strictly for black audiences!

The Heartbreak of Nitrate

There was little room in the warehouse for us to dismantle the entire stack and take an immediate inventory. That process had to wait until I could raise several hundred dollars to transport the films from the Tyler warehouse to a new warehouse in Dallas which had a special vault designed to keep such films cool, at a low humidity and which had a very sophisticated fire control system capable of coping with the highly-flammable nitrate should there ever be an accident. Isadore Roosth of Roosth and Genecov was kind enough to donate all the films to the Archives, and Dr. Eugene Bonelli, Dean of the Meadows School of Arts at Southern Methodist University, the Archives' home base, provided the funds for moving the films to their new home in Dallas.

By the fall of 1983, I knew that the collection contained over 100 short and feature films, of which thirty were prints of the black-audience films. Of these thirty, there were multiple copies of four of the films, making a total of twenty-two separate titles. Beyond the black-audience films, the rest of the collection was either standard Hollywood films of the same 1930s and 1940s period, or independent "exploitation" films, with titles like *Lash of the Penitentes*, *Swamp Girl*, or *Enlighten Thy Daughter*.

With only a few exceptions, all of the films were on the highly-flammable and delicate nitrate stock, with many of them in various stages of disintegration. Nitrate was used universally for 35-millimeter theatrical films until World War II. Nitrate's chemical composition is very close to the composition of gunpowder, and this sped up a transition to non-flammable acetate stock so that nitrate could go to war. By 1950, most theatrical films were printed on the new "safety stock," but the brilliance and visual depth of the old nitrate was lost forever to the screen. It was just as well, actually, because nitrate stock has a tendency to destroy itself. First, such films become covered with a fine, yellow-brown dust as the backing begins to break down. Then, the images

G. William Jones with Black Film Treasures and Lobby Cards

begin to stick to the next turn, so that unreeling the film does further damage (much as unrolling an ancient papyrus scroll does further damage to its precious contents). Finally, the film becomes a mixture of sticky, semi-solid masses awash in a puddle of dust. Estimates are that almost fifty percent of the world's pre-1950 film heritage is now gone forever—most of it to nitrate decomposition.

The Restoration Process

The Archives' next dilemma centered around trying to preserve the precious black-audience films from further disintegration. Checking with several film labs around the country, I found that the process of striking new negatives from the usable old prints, then pulling new 35-millimeter prints from the duplicate negatives would cost approximately $8,000 per feature black-and-white film, or $2,000 per ten-minute short film. Because the Southwest Film-Video Archives have merely made their home at S.M.U. for the past twenty years but have never been part of the University's budget, the only funds the Archives have ever received have been those raised through screenings, duplication fees for those titles which are in the public domain, donations and grants. It was a rare year when the Archives had as much as $6,000 in annual income. The cost of restoring only the black-audience films would run nearly $100,000, according to my estimate.

The Media Blitz

It all began with a modest little one-page press release from the Meadows School of the Arts publicity office. An enterprising young journalist from Tyler's *Courier Times Telegraph*, Ann Levin, came to Dallas to interview me, then made telephone interviews to other archives and to several film historians around the country. Her article about "the miraculous discovery of a long-lost chapter in black cultural history" prompted Peter Larson at the *Dallas Times-Herald* to do another, even longer article. In turn, Larson's article was picked up by the international press services, and a "media blitz" was on—a vortex of radio, television, newspaper and magazine interviews and stories which occupied most of my time in February of 1984.

I would like to be able to say that I was so smart that I planned to release the first news of my discovery on the eve of the nationwide Black History Month, knowing that the media would be avidly looking for news that was black, positive and—for television—visual. The discovery of the black-audience films cache was all of these things and I should have known that, after nearly twenty years of trying to get the media to be interested in the film events I had helped launch in

Dallas and at my university, including the highly-regarded U.S.A. Film Festival, this was the big opportunity. But, I have to admit that the dawn-to-midnight long distance calls, the visiting teams of commentators and their television crews, the trips to New York or Washington to be on "Nightline," "CBS Morning News," "Nightwatch," etc., the reams of newspaper and magazine clippings from all over the USA and even from Mexico, Canada and France—took me by delighted surpise.

The news about the films was on every television network, in every metropolitan and small town newspaper, in black readership magazines like *Ebony* and *Jet*, and even in a two-page spread in *Time* by film critic Richard Shickel. Almost every item broadcast the fact that I needed funds for restoration of the films, but it was not until an interview made locally was aired on National Public Radio—during morning drive-time when listeners were trapped in their cars on the expressways—that I got a call from the person who was to become the sponsor of our restoration project.

William Harris, Senior Vice-President of the Zale Jewelry Division of the Zale Corporation, called from the Zale home office in Dallas to say, "We want to help." Not dissuaded by news of the potential cost, he said, "I believe it will be worth it—to my company and to everyone concerned."

Finding a motion picture laboratory which would be the best one to do the difficult and exacting work of restoration and re-printing was my next chore. Most labs would not even think of accepting a reel of nitrate film through their front door. "No. Too dangerous," was their reply. Only four or five labs in the entire country would attempt to do the work. The one finally selected as the best for our purposes was in Pittsburgh. After we had selected our lab, there was trouble finding an interstate carrier which would transport nitrate films. Again we heard, "No. Too dangerous." Federal Express finally helped us out.

After meeting and overcoming numerous other obstacles, the "Tyler, Texas, Black Film Collection," as it became known, is now well on its way to being restored, with the first seven of the features and seven of the shorts now ready to be seen in a form as close as humanly possible to their original form. The decision as to which films to restore first was made only after an extensive search of other archives, through the American Film Institute and the Library of Congress, to determine which of our films were either the only known prints, the only prints in the original 35-millimeter format, or which measured out to be much longer than prints from other sources and were thus likely to be the most complete prints.

Given proper archival care, there is no good reason now why these restored films should not last as long as there are people who want to see them.

The Significance of the Collection

Most Americans, regardless of their ethnic background, seem to think that all-black-cast films began in the 1930s with *Hallelujah!*, *Cabin in the Sky*, *Stormy Weather* and *Green Pastures*. Although these titles were mostly well-made and were enjoyed to some degree by both white and black audiences of their time, they were Hollywood films which were made by white studio filmmakers and directed largely toward white audiences. Even before the all-white Biograph Company produced some of its ethnically-stereotyped films in the early teens, all-black-cast films were being made in Chicago by black independent filmmaker William Foster as early as 1910.

Most Americans, white or black, seem to think that black film-making began in 1969 when Gordon Parks, already a Pulitzer Prize winner for his work as a photographer for *Life* magazine wrote, pro-duced, and directed *The Learning Tree* for Warner Brothers-Seven Arts. Although this film was a milestone in terms of black artists gain-ing control of the Hollywood filmmaking process, it was made more than a half-century after the first black independent filmmakers began making films for segregated theaters in the South and de facto seg-regated theaters in the North. For four decades, there were as many as 1,200 theaters across the nation which played black-audience films either exclusively or on a preferential basis. Nineteen twenty-one was a peak year for distribution within this highly-organized and tightly-run production-distribution-exhibition system, which operated efficiently until its demise in the mid-fifties—as much through changing eco-nomic tides as through the growing sense that all-black theaters and films were no longer needed in the face of growing "integration." Dur-ing the forty-year span when black-audience films were in their heyday, few black artists other than the legendary Oscar Micheaux had their own production companies. Most of the companies were owned by white entrepreneurs who used white technicians behind their cameras. But a host of black producers, directors, and screenwriters— not to mention a multitude of black actors and actresses—had the opportunity to work on films which whites were never meant to see and in which, therefore, they could be truer to the realities of life as they experienced and felt them. Although we may still see some "stereotyping" in the films they made, it is not the ethnic stereotyping which marred many, if not most, of the Hollywood studio films of the same era. There was no need for such pandering to white prejudices, because the audience as well as the casts would be black.

Of the twenty-two separate titles represented in this collection, fifteen of them have a black artist as either producer, director, or screenwriter, and the majority of those have either a black writer-director or a black producer-director.

Thus, the "Tyler, Texas, Black Film Collection" is significant as testimony to the longer-than-supposed history of the black independent filmmaker in this country, as well as for providing one of the best sources for knowledge of the black self-consciousness in America from the mid-1930s through the mid-1950s.

The Non-White World of All-Black Cinema

One of the things that may strike us about American cinema is that, although a large percentage of our population is made up of black citizens, there are very few black people to be seen in most of our films. The fantasy world represented by American cinema is, largely, a world populated only by whites.

It is, then, perhaps dramatic justice that the opposite is true of most of the films made in America for black audiences. Except for some of the films of Oscar Micheaux, the fantasy world represented in the black-audience films is a world populated only by blacks. Micheaux, in his silent films as well as in his later sound films, was accustomed to dealing with such black/white issues as lynching, "passing," and intermarriage. There was no way in which he could avoid casting the occasional white person. But other black writer-director-producers, particularly in the sound era, were concerned mainly with giving their audiences a good time—an escapist entertainment—and the vicarious experience of a world without whites must have offered a deliciously enjoyable experience. The only trouble for black filmmakers with the all-black world they presented is that when they decided to depict realistically any of the troubles of black society, they either were restricted to presenting only those problems which arose between blacks without regard to whites, or their "villain" had to be an off-stage ghost.

Similarly, since its beginnings, much of film comedy has depended upon finding a "butt" for the humorous screen antics, and in a fantasy world populated only by blacks, the butts of the humor necessarily had to be black.

White Stereotypes/Black Stereotypes

Black screen actors, authors, directors, and producers have gotten so little attention over the near-century of film history that it is highly ironic, when we do finally see a "Black Film Festival," that the program is composed almost entirely of Hollywood films which were made by whites and for whites. Well into the 1950s, it was a rare Hollywood film which presented black characters at all, and even rarer when the characters were not stereotyped as dumb-but-loyal servants or as entertainers. They were included in films as objects of derision or diversion, but hardly ever as having serious, fully-formed lives with which audiences were invited to empathize. Such stereotyping and objectification possibly served to maintain a distance between whites and blacks which had been traditional since days of slavery. But, sad to report, even the black-made films which had little or no interference from white backers had their own share of stereotypes, too.

"Black is beautiful" is a sentiment which, apparently, had not yet been discovered when most of these films were made. Actors with light-colored skins, straightened hair and "Aryan" looks tended to have the leading and romantic roles, while the more dark-skinned, kinky-haired actors with more "African" looks usually played the comic, parental, or less important roles. This tends to be true regardless of whether the films' writers, producers, and directors are white or black.

Other stereotypes, which may have arisen from whites but seem to have been absorbed by blacks to some degree, are seen in such films as Spencer Williams' *Juke Joint*, in which the father is a lazy good-for-nothing while the mother is the more serious authority figure and the mainstay of the family.

Similarly, drinking, gambling, and fighting are the characteristic pastimes of any "low-life" characters in these films. Regardless of the real presence of honky-tonks and the numbers racket in many black communities of the time, plus frustrations which must often have boiled over into violence as they might have in any sector of a depressed and deprived community, the presence of these images in the black-made films leads, in today's screenings, to a low level of audience uneasiness. Nevertheless, this uneasiness is hardly comparable to that felt in viewing the more overtly-prejudiced Hollywood films of the same times.

It is refreshing when some of these stereotypes are presented, only to be made fun of and turned against themselves, as when, in *Souls Of Sin*, the bartender comes after a rowdy patron with his razor. In this case, though, the "weapon" is a harmless safety razor rather than the expected straight razor.

Black stereotypes in the old made-by-whites-for-whites Hollywood films indicate either naïveté or downright ethnic prejudice on the part of their makers. But similar stereotypes in made-by-blacks-for-black audiences may, perhaps, lead us to more sympathetic conclusions. When black life for two centuries had been dominated by white authority, when "white was right" and every media-distributed statement about American society flowed from the white media-makers, how could black folk have resisted being influenced by some of the white attitudes toward themselves, even though they were unfair, untrue, and repugnant? "Brainwashing" may have developed as a fine science only during the Korean War, but it operated in U.S. society long before the early 1950s.

Another question we must ask about stereotyping in any films is: Does it issue out of an unwillingness to take black life seriously, sympathetically? Or does it seem to come from black artists trying to represent their people sympathetically but realistically, with as much objectivity as they could be expected to muster as creatures of their own times, during their own times?

The "Crossovers"

One of the questions which comes up repeatedly following the screenings of these films is, "Were there many—or any—of the stars in these black-audience films who also managed to find work in the mainline, white-dominated film industry?"

The answer is, of course, yes. Many of the black actors and actresses who achieved international fame on the silver screen had their first exposure in some humble, low-budget film intended for mostly black audiences. Paul Robeson, the world's most famous black artist for several decades, played his first film role in Oscar Micheaux's *Body and Soul*. Lena Horne became a movie actress in the white producers Harry and Leo Popkins' *The Duke Is Tops*, which, after Lena made a big hit in several later Hollywood films, was re-titled *Bronze Venus*. Clarence Brooks, after starring in many of Lincoln and Micheaux motion picture companies' silent films, went on to play one of the first serious major black roles in a Hollywood film, as a Jamaican doctor in John Ford's 1931 adaptation of Sinclair Lewis's *Arrowsmith*. And Juano Hernandez, who distinguished himself as the noble black defendant in 1949s *Intruder in the Dust,* appeared in Oscar Micheaux's *Notorious Elinor Lee* in 1940. Many black comedians such as Stepin Fetchit and Mantan Moreland shuttled back and forth between Hollywood and wherever the black-audience films were being made, making far less money in the black-audience films but willing to trade the money, apparently, for better roles and billing in the smaller-budget films. Many musicians such as Cab Calloway, Louis Jordan, Count Basie, and Nat "King" Cole also had their first exposure on the screens of black theaters. These are only a few of the black artists who had their screen debuts in black-audience films and then graduated to the mainstream Hollywood pictures.

One of the great losses which occurred when the black-audience films died out in the early 1950s was the destruction of a much-needed portal through which black artists could pass into worldwide fame.

Vive La Différance!

Seeing the black-audience films today, as when they were seen in their original releases, the first thing which strikes us about them is likely to be their technical and even artistic crudeness when compared to Hollywood films of the same years. They definitely look "home-made" by comparison. But when we take into account that the average budget for even a B-grade formula Western was in the hundreds of thousands of dollars while few films for black audiences ever cost more than $25,000, much of the blame for the crudeness falls upon the size of the budgets rather than upon the artistic abilities and sensibilities of the black filmmakers. With such low budgets, the basic miracle to be applauded is that the films are in focus and that the splices hold! After that, any kind of effective humor, drama and relevant social commentary is pure profit for the audiences.

Readers can find for themselves in the synopses of the films which follow which films make what relevent contributions. What may not come through on the printed page, however, is the comparative warmth and ease of viewing black actors in these films as opposed to seeing them in the Hollywood films of the same decades. While viewing King Vidor's *Hallelujah!* or the William Keighley/Marc Connelly production of *Green Pastures*—two of the most highly-reputed black-cast Hollywood films of the early sound days—one is torn between appreciating the fine performances of the actors and cringing at the harsh and unwarranted ethnic stereotyping which comes, wave after wave, upon us. By contrast, the black-audience films have a certain palpable "family feeling" because they were never meant to be seen by white eyes and could be almost as expressive of the black realities of the times as they wanted to be without fear that some projectionist was going to cut an offending scene from the reel or that the film would be picketed by the Klan—or worse.

If the black-audience films have any benefit and relevance to contemporary audiences, it lies rather obviously not in their esthetic values but in the fact that they may help fill a glaring gap in the history of American independent filmmaking, and in the fact that they give us one of the richest and most revealing commentaries on how black people saw themselves and their world during the years in which they were made.

Some Pioneer Black Filmmakers

Since 1965, history books about motion pictures have proliferated. There are now hundreds of books about the rise and development of cinema. In most of these books, certain names such as Griffith, Eisenstein, Von Stroheim, Wyler, Walsh, Murnau, Bergman, Fellini, and Renoir appear again and again as their contributions to the twentieth century's most characteristic art are chronicled. There are even books about the great "B" movies and their directors, as well as one or two about the famous "turkeys" of all times.

But a reader will look far and wide for even one word in these books about the black filmmakers of the 1910s through the early 1950s who labored against gigantic odds to make independent films for black audiences. Although they produced vibrant moving images of their own people and times and explored new reaches of low-budget financing, filming, and distribution that Hollywood filmmakers of their times would have sworn were impossible, these black filmmakers have remained largely anonymous in the decades since we have been paying attention to the only new artform mankind has been able to come up with since pre-historic times. (For the few fine books which do pay well-deserved attention to these neglected artists, see Appendix Two.)

Here, then, are brief biographies and filmographies of some of these pioneers. The ones celebrated in these pages are by no means the only black filmmakers of those times, but only the ones whose work is represented in the Tyler, Texas, Black Film Collection.

The Dean of Black Filmmakers (1884–1951)

Oscar Micheaux was a man who fought the odds all of his life. Even if he was not always a winner, he was always a contender. He simply saw no good reason why he could not do something anyone else was able to do, as long as he wanted to do it badly enough. It did not particularly matter to him whether those others were black or white—if they could do it, so could he.

It all seems to have started when he became, at the age of twenty-five, one of the rare black homesteaders out in South Dakota. He had already had a turn at being a bootblack and then a Pullman porter, but he had bigger dreams to fulfill. In South Dakota, he did not have many neighbors, and all he had were white. He learned to get along with them and with the land so well that, by the time he had been on his land only five years, he had expanded his holdings to 500 acres under plow. Another itch had taken hold of him during his fourth year as a homesteader—probably during the winter, when there was little to do on the windswept, snow-covered prairie but read books.

He decided that he wanted to write a book.

No matter that there were very few black authors getting published at the time. And, when he had finished his manuscript, no matter that he could not find a publisher who would print it into a book and then distribute it as widely as possible. With his own money, he published the book himself and then he got into his car and covered every backroad and every navigable wagon track, selling his book door-to-door to the white farmers and small businessmen in the tiny towns. The book was named *The Homesteader*, and it was about what those farmers knew: being a homesteader in a hard land. Oscar talked their language well enough to sell them the book, and he wrote it well enough for them to like the book and to assure himself that he could be a successful writer.

So, in 1915, when he lost his homestead (later, he claimed it was due to financial malfeasance of his father-in-law, a minister), Micheaux moved to Sioux City, Iowa, where he established the Western Book and Supply Company. He continued writing his novels, publishing them himself and touring the countryside to sell them, one at a time.

Not far away, in Lincoln, Nebraska, George P. Johnson got hold of a

Oscar Micheaux (right) playing a detective in his film Murder in Harlem.

second-hand copy of *The Homesteader*. George was the general booking manager for the western states of the Lincoln Motion Picture Company of Los Angeles, and in the book he saw the possibilities of a good film for his company.

The Lincoln Company had been producing films strictly for black audiences for the past three years, with some success. Johnson's brother, Noble, had been acting in motion pictures for several years at Universal Studios and had been running the Lincoln studio in Los Angeles while George did the booking business from Nebraska, while also working full-time as a mailman.

Whether Micheaux had already been dreaming of being a film producer before Johnson summoned him to a conference in Lincoln is not known, but by the time Micheaux had spent two days living at Johnson's house and discussing terms for the sale of his book, it was obvious that this was the author's next dream. He said to the Johnson brothers, "You can make a motion picture of my book, but only on the condition that I direct it."

Thinking that Micheaux was an upstart, and knowing that he had no prior experience with any aspect of filmmaking, the Johnsons turned him down and dropped the project. But Oscar did not drop the project. Instead, he returned to Sioux City, re-organized his business into the Micheaux Film and Book Company, and began to raise money for his own film of his own book.

He went to those he knew best—the farmers and small businessmen in and around Sioux City, offering them stock in his new venture for from $75 to $100 per share. The people believed in him, and before the end of that year he had raised enough to begin production on his first film, *The Homesteader*, which was not a timid one- or two-reeler, but a full eight-reel feature. When, in early 1919, the film was finished, he took a leaf from the Johnson brothers' book and distributed the film the same way they did, but with his own personal flair for public relations. With a print of the film and advertising material under his arm, he would travel from city to city, in ever-widening circles, to hit up each theater owner with a proposition for showing his film. At the same time, he would tell them the story and show them a few photos of stars for his next film, encouraging them to pay a little something up-front for exclusive rights to show the completed feature the next year. In between times, he would continue to sell his growing backlog of novels, still door-to-door.

In this manner, Micheaux managed to produce thirty films over the next ten years. The decade of the 1920s was when films made for predominately black audiences in theaters across the country which catered primarily to black patrons had their highest levels of success until the "Blaxploitation" era of the 1970s. It was in that decade Oscar Micheaux went from being an unknown upstart who had the crazy idea he could make movies to being the head of the most respected (and often disrespected), most successful, and most enduring black-owned film production company during the entire 1910–1956 era of black independent filmmaking.

If Oscar Micheaux had wanted general acclaim, honor, and peace of mind, he would never have made more than one motion picture. From the beginning, he stood at the center of a vortex of controversy, censorship, and financial problems. Although some of his black critics, both then and now, accused him of producing films designed only to make a profit but not to elevate his ethnic group in their own or others' eyes, he usually disdained to make films which were purely and simply escapism. Had he chosen to emulate some of the later black filmmakers of the forties (and most of the white filmmakers who made films for black audiences at that time) and produced only frothy musicals, comedies, Westerns, and gangster films which were merely black copies of then-current Hollywood fare, Micheaux could probably have made much more money, could have saved a lot of time spent in re-working his films to suit various censorship boards, and might have actually been given more respect from film critics on both black and white newspapers. But Micheaux obviously believed in choosing uniquely black themes for his uniquely black audiences, thinking that these themes would be infinitely more interesting to them. Thus, he was to make film after film on the themes of black persons "passing" for white, intermarriage between blacks and whites, the ubiquitous plagues of the numbers and prostitution rackets, injustice of the white courts against blacks, and even the potentially dangerous issues of lynching and the vigilante depredations of the Ku Klux Klan.

Few viewers of his work, then or now, would say that Oscar Micheaux made the most artistic of the black-produced independent films. Micheaux productions suffered under the same financial and personnel restrictions faced by other black production companies of his time: Lincoln, Ebony, Reol, Arista, etc. Few of the companies were able to muster more than $15,000 for a feature film, and all of them had to use white union cameramen and editors, who were paid the same union wages they would have gotten if they had been working in a Hollywood studio. (One big reason why there were no black camera operators or editors in those years is because the unions would not yet accept black applicants for membership.) But whereas other black producers might hone their scripts to a finer point before going into the studio to shoot them, do a few re-takes in order to get a particular shot just right or hire a really good editor to "save in the editing room" some mistakes made in shooting, Oscar Micheaux was like a racehorse who—once the starting-bell rings—is intent only upon reaching the finishing-line. Once a production began, he had neither the time nor the interest for re-shooting a scene in which the light was too low or the actors fluffed their lines slightly. ("Print it!" must have been used instead of "Cut!" at the end of each shot.) Similarly, he had little use for the expensive and time-consuming work of creating just the right, original "mood" music or for the painstaking and meticulous jobs of fine-tuning the editing so that scenes flowed together with a pacing and tempo that underscored the acting.

In defense of Micheaux's style of filmmaking, it should be said that very few black independent filmmakers had the time or money to do better, and that Micheaux never gave himself the luxury of doing one thing at a time. Although he might be on the set for the day's shooting, he was—at the same time—working on the script or on financial arrangements for his next film, getting ready to go on the road to distribute the film now shooting when it was completed, and going over receipts of past Micheaux Corporation films with his brother and chief accountant, Swan. Other companies tended to let some other entity handle their financing and distribution, to make only one film per year and to go out of business after their first or second film.

In the early 1930s, the Micheaux Corporation was the only independent black filmmaking company to survive not only the influenza epidemic but also the earliest and harshest years of the Great Depression and the coming of sound to film. The company did not come through unscathed, however. Micheaux's old company went bankrupt and he had to re-form it and—for the first time—fall back upon white financiers rather than raising the money himself. But the films of Oscar Micheaux were to continue in much the same style, and with much of the same difficulties and controversy, until his last production in 1948.

Three years later, Oscar Micheaux died. Like many other motion picture pioneers before him—Georges Melies in France and David Wark Griffith in the United States, to name only a couple—he died unnoticed and uncelebrated. None of his silent films except *Body and Soul* survive today, and not all of his sound films.

It has only been since the 1970s that much attention, black or white, has been paid to the phenomenon of the black-audience films and their makers, 1910 through 1956, and only since that time has Oscar Micheaux been tardily celebrated with his rightful title of "The Father of Independent Black Filmmaking." In 1987, the "Avenue of the Stars" in Hollywood finally dedicated a star on its sidewalk to Oscar Micheaux.

The Films of Oscar Micheaux

1919: *The Homesteader*
1920: *Phantom of Kenwood, Swing, Dark Princess, A Fool's Errand, Within Our Gates*

1921: *The Hypocrite, The Shadow, The Symbol of the Unconquered, The Gunsaulus Mystery*

1922: *The Dungeon, Uncle Jasper's Will*

1923: *Ghost of Tolston's Manor, Deceit, Virgin of the Seminole*

1924: *Son of Satan, Birthright*

1925: *Body amd Soul, Marcus Garland, The Brute*

1926: *The Devil's Disciple, The Conjure Woman*

1927: *The Spider's Web, The Millionaire, The Broken Violin, The House Behind the Cedars*

1928: *Thirty Years Later, When Men Betray*

1929: *Wages of Sin*

1930: *Easy Street, Daughter of the Congo*

1931: *The Exile, Darktown Review*

1932: *Veiled Aristocrats, Ten Minutes to Live, Black Magic*

1933: *The Girl From Chicago, Ten Minutes to Kill*

1934: *Harlem After Midnight*

1935: *Lem Hawkins' Confession*

1936: *Underworld, Temptation*

1937: *God's Stepchildren*

1939: *Lying Lips*

1940: *The Notorious Elinor Lee*

1948: *Betrayed*

SPENCER WILLIAMS
(1893–1969)

Although he was best known to the general American public in his role as "Andy Brown," which he played in the early (and short-lived) television adaptation of "Amos n' Andy," the talents and accomplishments of Spencer Williams went far beyond that role. In the 1930s, his was the only voice inside the Hollywood studios which spoke out—and wrote—for any view of black life other than the current white stereotyped interpretation. In the 1940s, Williams became one of the most prolific and respected writer-director-actors in black-audience films, with nine feature films to his directorial credit.

Born on July 14, 1893, in Vidalia, Louisiana, he managed to get himself to New York City around 1910, where he landed a job as a "call boy" for the great Oscar Hammerstein and later studied acting and

Spencer Williams, far right, was probably best known for his role as Andy in the television series "Amos n' Andy."

the art of comedy from none other than Bert Williams, with whom he had become friends.

After several years of service in the U. S. Army during World War I, Spencer Williams next entered the public eye—or, rather, the public ear—in his one-and-only venture as a recording artist. Williams and Lonnie Jackson recorded a vocal duet of "It Feels So Good," which was released on the Okeh Race Records label.

When Hollywood went crazy over talking pictures soon after *The Jazz Singer*, the studios began to scour the New York talent and technical pool for anybody who knew anything about sound. In a manner which was to become characteristic with Williams but uncharacteristic of other black artists of the time, Williams signed on with the old Christie Studios in Hollywood not as on-camera talent but as a behind-the-camera sound technician. The first equipment for making "talkies" at the Christie Studios was installed with the help of Williams.

Always looking for an opportunity to improve his status, he was soon noticed by the studio head, Al Christie, who realized that Williams could add a note of authenticity to a series of black-cast comedies which were to be adaptations of some of the stories of Jewish writer Octavus Roy Cohen. When Cohen and the Christie troupe went South to film "authentic" location shots for the comedy series, Spencer Williams went along as co-writer with Cohen. Although he was employed mainly to write dialogue that would sound appropriate in the mouths of the black actors, it is known that Williams was soon having an influence upon Cohen and his story-lines, resulting in the production of several comedies in the series which were much more true to black self-concepts than they would have been had Cohen been the sole writer. Before long, Williams was not only writing the scripts, but also acting in some of them, such as *The Melancholy Dame*, *Oft in the Silly Night*, *The Lady Fare*, *Music Hath Harms*, and *The Framing of the Shrew*. Various sources give Williams credit for also having directed some of the films in the series, such as *Tenderfeet* and *The Melancholy Dame*, and it is possible that he did perform such services, but the Library of Congress copyright files record that white director Archie Mayo was given credit for directing *Tender Feet* while Arvid E. Gillstrom was listed as director for *The Melancholy Dame*. Although the Christie series was designed primarily for white audiences and contained ethnic stereotyping that would be repugnant to many viewers both white and black of today, the films are significant in that they did present much authentic black lore of the times (most of it probably from Williams' pen) and in that a good part of the series films which were released in 1928 were actually the first black talkies, rather than Metro-Goldwyn-Mayer's *Hallelujah!* and Fox's *Hearts in Dixie*, which some records mistakenly identify as the first all-black-cast talking pictures. Regardless of any such confusions, it is clear that Spencer Williams played a large and important part in the creation of these relatively early depictions of black life-style, flawed though they might appear to us today when we are able to see them.

Through the 1930s, Spencer Williams continued to write and act for films, mostly for those with all-black casts which were designed for all-black audiences. He had roles in *Georgia Rose*, *Virginia Judge*, and *Bad Boy* as well as appearing—usually as a villain—in almost every one of the "black Westerns," including *Bronze Buckaroo*, *Harlem Rides the Range*, *Two-gun Man from Harlem*, and *Harlem on the Prairie*. In 1937, he acted in and wrote the script for the first all-black-cast talking horror film, *Son of Ingagi*.

It was the 1940s, however, that were to be Williams' real heyday be-hind the camera. Teaming up with a Jewish film entrepreneur named Alfred Sack who operated Sack Amusement Enterprises out of Dallas, Williams was able to find in Sack a hands-off backer who enabled him to do what few other black artists other than Oscar Micheaux had been able to do—to direct a large number of his own screenplays as he saw fit. If Sack had any doubts at first about letting Williams have his own way on the set, the success that greeted *The Blood of Jesus*, Spencer Williams' first true experiment as a writer-director-actor, must have convinced the Dallas producer-distributor that it was just plain good business for Williams to call the shots. Thus began a ten-year associa-tion that produced three religious features (*The Blood of Jesus*, *Brother Martin*, and *Go Down, Death!*), three comedies (*Dirty Gertie from Harlem*, *U.S.A.*; *Beale Street Mama;* and *Juke Joint*), and three dramas (*Marchin' On*, *Of One Blood*, and *The Girl in Room 20*).

The Spencer Williams comedies still play well to audiences today, but especially those that feature the comedy team of Williams as "Bad News Johnson" and July Jones as his mugging sidekick. *Juke Joint* and *Beale Street Mama* exhibit a kind of black Laurel and Hardy team that leave viewers wishing the two had made more comic films together.

Although all of Williams' directorial efforts suffer from the usual technical problems characteristic of any extremely low-budget films (his entire budgets were usually around $12,000 to $15,000, amounts insufficient to produce even the trailers to most Hollywood studio features of the time), at least one modern black film critic, Thomas Cripps, calls *The Blood of Jesus* "an unrivalled example of black con-trol of the medium, with untrammelled expression of black religious sensitivity." In his book, *Black Film As Genre* (Indiana University Press, Bloomington, 1978), Cripps devotes the equivalent of an entire chapter to this film, so important does he think the film is as a prime example of how authentic a motion picture can be to black culture when it is made with as little as possible of white interference.

For Spencer Williams, the 1950s were to be a decade devoted to the new medium of television, but the time available for such devotion turned out to be all too short. In 1950, the Columbia Broadcasting System decided to experiment with turning the fantastically popular old radio series of "Amos n' Andy" into a television series—but with an important change. The radio series had been acted out by a team of white writer-actors who had created the roles, Freeman Gosden and Charles Correll. The team had also starred in one film version of the series in 1930 entitled *Check and Double Check*, playing their roles in burnt cork blackface. By 1950, CBS programmers were wise enough to know that blackface would no longer go down well with large numbers of American viewers, but why not shoot it with black actors and actresses in the roles? Spencer Williams was chosen to play the role of Andy Brown, which he did to the best of his considerable ability until the show was cancelled after the 1952–1953 season because of the vocal protests of, among others, the NAACP.

Although the early fifties established him as a familiar face in the homes of America, in terms of a black artist enabled to practice the fullest range of his talents, the forties were the Golden Age for Spencer Williams.

He died on December 13, 1969, at his home in Los Angeles at the age of seventy-six.

The Films of Spencer Williams (as Director)

1941: *The Blood of Jesus*
1942: *Brother Martin*
1943: *Marchin' On* (aka *Where's My Man Tonight?*)
1944: *Of One Blood, Go Down, Death!*
1946: *Dirty Gertie From Harlem, U.S.A., The Girl In Room 20, Beale Street Mama*
1947: *Juke Joint*

WILLIAM ALEXANDER
(1912(?)–   )

In the 1940s, most producers of black-audience films were white: Ted Toddy, Al Sack, Jack and Bert Goldberg, Arthur Dreifuss and Richard Kahn, to name a few. The producer, of course, is usually responsible for initiating a film: finding a script or at least a good idea, finding the sources of financing, employing screenwriter and director, etc. Aside from the work of the very prolific Oscar Micheaux in the twenties and thirties, there were very few black persons connected with motion pictures who had the ability—or the inclination, apparently—to perform these exacting and difficult roles. In the 1940s and 1950s, William Alexander was the most accomplished exception.

Alexander received his college education at Colorado State University and the University of Chicago. His first recorded entry into the field of motion pictures came in 1945, right after World War II, when he organized the Associated Producers of Negro Motion Pictures, Inc., in New York City. The purpose of this organization was to provide the platform from which he was to produce his first films, beginning with the 1946 releases of two short films, *The Highest Tradition* (about black people in the U.S. Army) and *The Call of Duty* (about black people in the U.S. Navy). Both of these films were documentaries, foreshadowing his later interest in producing newsreels.

In April and May of 1946, Alexander received some very favorable publicity in the *Los Angeles Sentinel* about his high sense of purpose in becoming a film producer. In April, he was quoted as saying: "If Negro films are to survive and attract larger audiences, new ideas will have to replace the often repeated stereotyped subjects now used."

The next month, the same newspaper reported that Alexander and his Associated Producers of Negro Motion Pictures planned production of a full-length feature "presenting Negroes in an intelligent and dignified manner, thus setting the pace for Hollywood to follow."

In his first year of releasing pictures, William Alexander changed the name of his company to Alexander Productions and premiered two other new short films; *Flicker Up*, a musical starring Billy Eckstine and Mary Lou Harris, and *Vanities*, in which a talented young impressionist, Charles Keith, emceed for musical numbers by Joesfred Portee and Audrey Armstrong.

William Alexander (right), interviewing J. Earnest Wilkins in one of his By-Line Newsreels.

Alexander's feature films began in 1947 with the release of the second film to star world champion prizefighter Joe Louis (the first had been *Spirit Of Youth* in 1937 by Grand National Films), entitled *The Fight Never Ends*. That year was Alexander's biggest, with three more features and a short following each other in rapid succession: *Jivin' in Bebop*, a feature-length record of the music of Dizzy Gillespie and his Band; *Love In Syncopation*, a fictionalized feature treatment of the story of Henri Woods and his Band and their rise to fame from beginnings in the Seabees; *That Man Of Mine*, another musical starring Ruby Dee, Powell Lindsay and Henri Woods and his Six Hepcats.

Although *The Fight Never Ends* (1946) still receives favorable comment as a sincere and authentic representation of black achievement, it was probably Alexander's 1949 release, *Souls of Sin*, which epitomized the ambitions he voiced to the *Los Angeles Sentinel* as he began his producing career. Actors William Greaves, Jimmy Wright, and Emery Richardson, under the direction of Powell Lindsay (who also played the villain of the film) presented a realistic panorama of black lifestyles in the Harlem of the 1940s, from a burned-out failure of a writer to an angry but determined con-man to a young innocent full of talent.

Although his work in production of features and musical shorts is still impressive, the world may credit him most in years to come as the producer of the *By-Line Newsreel* series, from 1953 to 1956. Appearing himself in the role of the interviewer and serving also as the off-camera narrator, Alexander roved the country in the earliest years of the Civil Rights Amendment's implementation, recording the great strides which black people were making in the armed forces and in the federal government. At a time when black faces and accomplishments were still very rare in the major-studio newsreels, William Alexander was capturing on film an era of accomplishment and position for blacks which had not been seen since Reconstruction.

Perhaps because of contacts he made as a newsreel producer in Washington, Alexander moved his base of operations in the late fifties to London, from whence he spent more than a decade making documentary films for some of the emerging nations of Africa.

In 1973, to cap (so far, because he is still very much alive and at work today) his producing career, Alexander was called to Hollywood to co-produce (with Bill Shiffin) a major film project for Paramount Pictures entitled *The Klansman*, which boasted of Samuel Fuller and Millard Kaufman as screenwriters, Terence Young as director and Richard Burton, Lee Marvin, Lola Falana, and O. J. Simpson as actors. The film, set in backwoods Alabama, was about a sheriff who contradicts red-necked accusations of blacks in the rape of a white woman and ends up confronting the Ku Klux Klan. As is often the case in the art/business of motion pictures, the fertile and expensive gathering of talents did not, finally, succeed in giving birth to a great example of cinematic art or of humanistic truth. *Variety's* review said, "There's not a shred of quality, dignity, relevance or impact in this yahoo-oriented bunk," and the film was a failure at the box office. Apparently, even though he was the project's producer, William Alexander was finally unable to give the 1974 production the kind of simple insight and tone of sincerity he had achieved with an apparently much less promising array of talent—and only a fraction of the budget—with *Souls of Sin* in 1949.

The Films of William Alexander (as Producer)

1946: *The Highest Tradition, The Call of Duty, Flicker Up* (aka *Rhythm in A Riff*), *Vanities*

1947: *The Fight Never Ends, Jivin' in Bebop, Love in Syncopation, That Man of Mine, Sweethearts of Rhythm*
1949: *Souls of Sin*
1953–1956: *By-Line Newsreels*
1974: *The Klansman*

GEORGE RANDOL

(1895–?)

Although George Randol was involved as producer on only three films during the heyday of black-audience films, his career is important in the history of black independent filmmaking, not only because he is one of the few black artists ever to succeed in the difficult tasks surrounding the job of producer in feature films, but also because of the importance of the film he co-directed with Ralph Cooper, *Dark Manhattan*.

Born in Virginia in 1895, Randol received his public school education in Rankin, Pennsylvania and in Cleveland, Ohio. He graduated from the Cleveland School of Music with a degree in Voice Culture, and became a private pupil of Professor Walter T. Gerak of St. Louis.

As a singer, his first public appearance was with the Thomas Male Quartet in Helena, Montana. His career was briefly interrupted by World War I, in which he served as a second lieutenant with the 349th Artillery in France. After the war, he returned to the States and soon was playing featured roles in such Broadway musicals as *How Come?* (in which Eddie Hunter was then starring) and Irvin C. Miller's *Models*, in which he played the male lead. He also played the role of the Pharoah in the stage version of *Green Pastures*.

In 1934, he toured the U. S. and Canada as a concert singer; but by 1936, George Randol was seeking his future within the movie colony of Hollywood, possibly inspired to do so by the example of Oscar Micheaux. Randol had gotten to know the great "Father of Black Filmmaking" through being hired to play a role in Micheaux's first talking film, *The Exile*, in 1931. He met Ralph Cooper, who was then a contract actor with Twentieth Century-Fox, playing a wide assortment of villainous roles. Of their meeting of minds, Randol was later to say, "We were tired of seeing our fine stars playing small, distasteful parts in the many films released by the major film companies, so we insisted upon better scripts and parts for our players and we got pushed around, so that we decided to write and produce our own."

It was still in 1936 that Randol and Cooper—feeling that the major studios were not going to give black actors a chance at the better roles—teamed up to form the Cooper-Randol Production Company and began work on their first (and only) co-production. With a script in hand entitled *Dark Manhattan*, they rented space in the old Grand-National Studios near the intersection of Hollywood Boulevard and Fountain Avenue and began production. The story concerned the rise of "Curly" Thorpe (played by Cooper himself) to the position of kingpin of the Harlem numbers racket, and was pretty much a black version of the major studios' gangster films then in vogue.

The premiere of the picture, which was scheduled for Los Angeles' Tivoli Theatre on January 27, 1937, had to be delayed because Randol, Cooper, and their partners could not come up with $13,000 in processing charges to get the film out of the lab. (This was almost the entire cost of the film.) But finally, six weeks after the film's completion, the money was found and *Dark Manhattan* premiered at the Tivoli on February 13, 1937.

Surely Randol and Cooper expected their film to be successful, but it is probable that neither of them could have known just how important it would be. Black-audience films, after experiencing their peak of popularity in the latter days of silent movies, were hard-hit by the greater expenses involved in making sound films. Then, the Depression came, and dealt a death blow to almost all the producers of these films. Few of the black independent filmmakers were to survive this double crisis. But the fresh and imaginative style of *Dark Manhattan*, coupled with the fact that it began an exciting new genre of black-cast gangster films, made the film such a surprising success that it started a resurgence in the production of films for black audiences. In the following six or seven years, more than a dozen gangster films were made, seeking to copy the format and the success of *Dark Manhattan*.

Soon after they had experienced success, however, Randol and Cooper parted ways—Cooper to join with white entrepreneurs Harry and Leo Popkin to create Million Dollar Films, and Randol to organize his own Premiere Productions, a name he soon changed to George Randol Productions.

Randol decided to begin his career as a solo producer by making a relatively inexpensive short film which must have been his attempt to combine two types of films then enjoying success with black audiences: musicals and Westerns. While preparing for the film, he worked for Associated Pictures as the Sheriff in *Harlem on the Prairie*, so he was familiar with the Western formula. Taking his cast of Troy Brown, the Jackson Brothers, Rosalie Lincoln, and Jim Davis on location to the old Lasky Ranch outside Los Angeles, Randol shot his film. It was released in 1938 as *Rhythm Rodeo*.

With one solo production under his belt, he was now ready to begin making films in earnest. With several scripts in mind, he formed an organization to sell shares in his company, sending his salesmen out with these words for potential backers:

"There are more than 600 theatres in this country which cater mainly to colored people for support. Statistics show that we can realize a profit of $60,000 for a picture that costs $15,000 to make. We think this money should be returned to the pockets of the people who spend it for their entertainment."

His salesmen were effective enough to raise the $15,000 necessary for Randol to begin producing his first feature film on his own, *Midnight Shadow*, which was an unusual mixture of romance, murder mystery, and comedy starring Frances Webb, Buck Woods, Clinton Rosemond, and Ruby Dandridge. As he had with *Rhythm Rodeo*, Randol not only filled the role of the producer, but also the slots of screenwriter and director.

After the release of *Midnight Shadow*, Randol announced to the trade press that he was merging his George Randol Productions with the Argus Film Company and the Ernest Steiss Film Company. His future productions were to be distributed by Bert Goldberg's International Road Shows, Inc. Although it must have seemed like a mutually-beneficial alliance at the time, promising to put an end to many of Randol's fund raising problems, no more films were forthcoming. *Midnight Shadow* was George Randol's last film.

Leaving Hollywood and the burdens of a film producer behind him, Randol returned to Broadway, where he was to play numerous parts and to have the opportunity to use his fine singing voice once more. In

1945, he received good response from the critics for his role in *Anna Lucasta*.

The Films of George Randol (as Producer)

1937: *Dark Manhattan* (co-produced)
1938: *Rhythm Rodeo*
1939: *Midnight Shadow*

IV

The Tyler, Texas, Black Film Collection

The following synopses and photographs are from those films in the "Tyler, Texas, Black Film Collection" which have so far been saved to safety film from their deteriorating condition on nitrate film. Most of the photographs are "frame blow-ups" from the original nitrate prints.

Although some of these films have been mentioned in previous studies of the independent black-audience film phenomenon, in most cases the researchers were apparently unable actually to view the films, but relied on newspaper critiques or press exploitation materials printed at the time of the films' first release. Because of reliance upon such secondary sources, much of their information is either extremely abbreviated or, in some cases, incorrect. In an effort to give future researchers a firmer base for their studies and to inform the general reading public of the actual content of these films, extended and illustrated synopses of the films' story-lines or documentary coverage are included here.

The Blood of Jesus

CREDITS

Director: Spencer Williams
Producer: Alfred Sack/Sack Amusement Enterprises
Cinematographer: Jack Whitman
Sound: R. E. Byers
Screenplay: Spencer Williams
Music: Rev. R. L. Robertson and the Heavenly Choir
Year of Release: 1941
Running Time: 68 minutes (6,065 ft.)

CAST

Ras Jackson: Spencer Williams
Martha Jackson: Cathryn Caviness
Sister Jenkins: Juanita Riley
Sister Ellerby: Heather Hardeman
The Angel: Rogenia Goldthwaite
Satan: James B. Jones
Judas Green: Frank H. McClennan
Rufus Brown: Eddie DeBuse
Luke Willows: Alva Fulle

SYNOPSIS

Accompanied by the Heavenly Choir's singing of "Good News!" and "Go Down, Moses," we see a humble plowman tilling his fields (in a sequence which Director Williams borrowed from a previous film entitled *Broken Earth*) while Narrator Williams tells us:

"Almost gone are the days when Peace ruled the earth with a firm and gentle hand, when fear of God dwelt in the hearts of men and women and children, when the Ten original Command-

Martha is baptised.

Ras realizes he has accidently shot Martha.

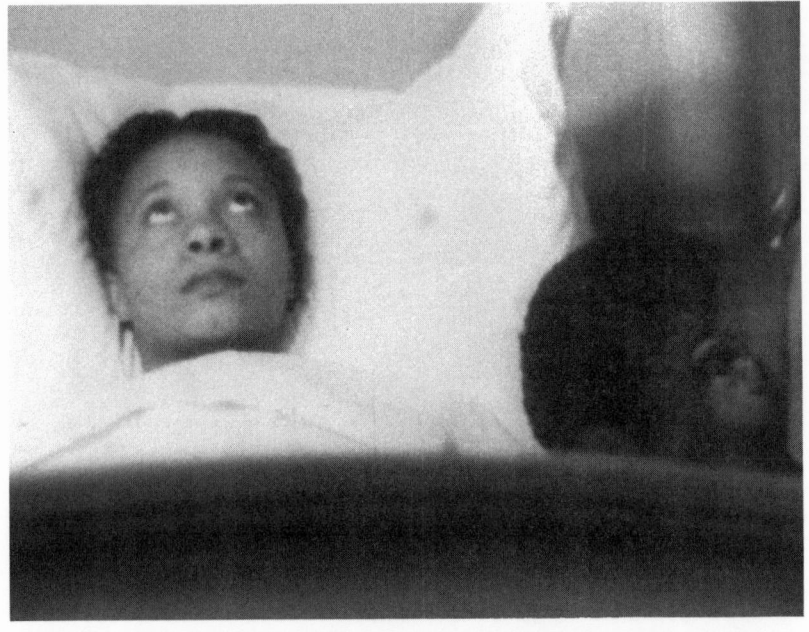

As Ras kneels at Martha's side, the congregation prays.

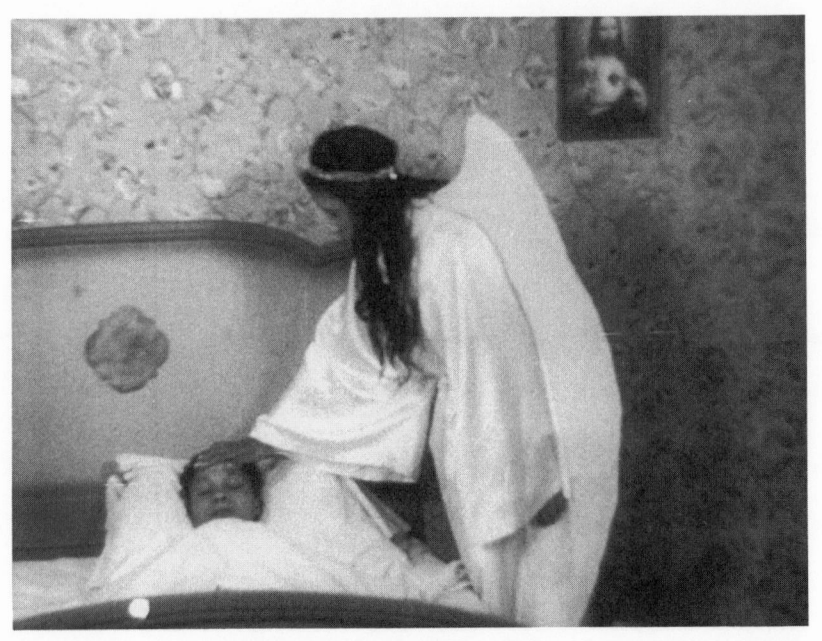

The angel bids Martha's spirit to rise.

Satan tells Judas to lead Martha astray.

Martha escapes from the roadhouse.

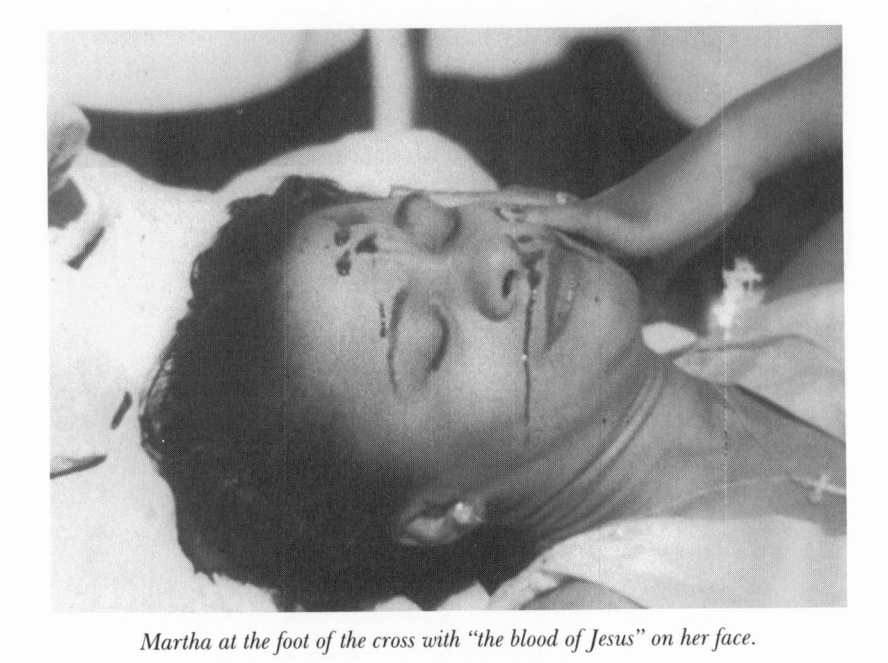

Martha at the foot of the cross with "the blood of Jesus" on her face.

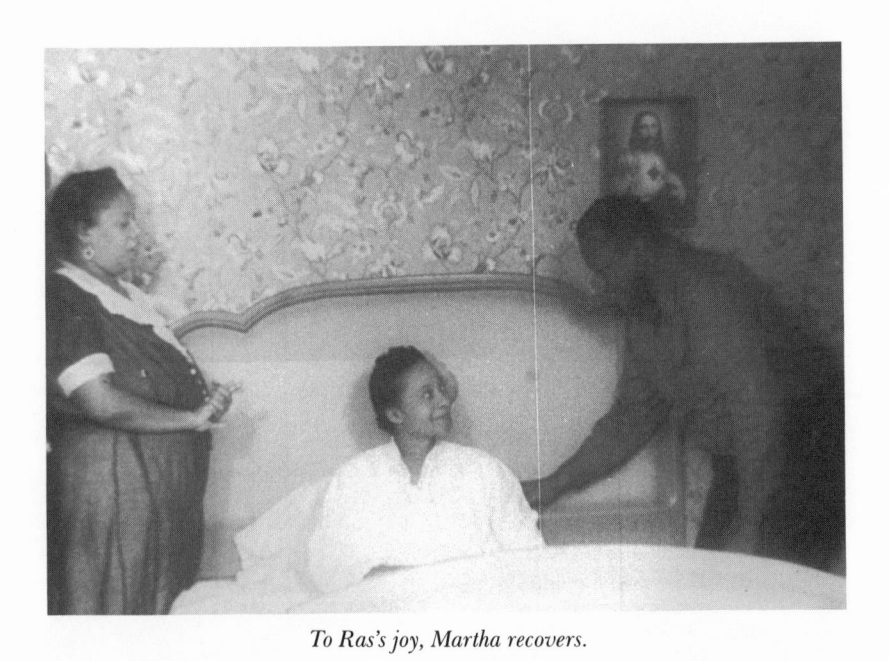

To Ras's joy, Martha recovers.

ments were the accepted laws of every civilized country and nation on the face of the globe, when those who prayed on their knees in church on Sunday did not go back to their homes to prey on their neighbors the remaining six days of the week, when religion was practiced with unfalse solemnity and honest sincerity, and when souls' salvation was a heritage from Heaven to not merely a few thousands but to many millions. Those days are almost gone from the earth—almost—"

A rural congregation, some of its members dressed in white robes, makes its way down to the riverside as we hear "All God's Children Got Shoes." Once there, the Song Leader phrases out "On Jordan's Stormy Banks I Stand" and then "Amazing Grace."

During the singing, two of the congregation—Sister Jenkins and Sister Ellerby—comment about their doubts that Sister Jackson, waiting to be baptized, really "has religion." They suspect any failings she has may be caused by her husband, Ras. Married only three months, Ras hasn't even bothered to come see his wife baptized, but has gone hunting instead!

The Preacher is frustrated in trying to baptize Luke Willows because Luke thinks he sees a snake in the water. Finally, he breaks away from the brothers, unbaptized, and makes his escape (to the tune of the Heavenly Choir's "Run, Child, Run"). One of the congregation wryly remarks that it was an alligator Luke thought he saw at last year's baptizing.

When Martha Jackson is baptized, it is Sister Jenkins who goes to wrap her up in a robe and see her home.

At the Jackson house, after Sister Jenkins has helped Martha into dry clothes and persuaded her to lie down awhile, she meets Ras on the front porch.

Seeing the bulging burlap bag, she asks Ras, "You have any luck?"

"Just a couple of rabbits, that's all," he says, nervously.

The sack looks too big and heavy to her to contain only rabbits, but Ras keeps insisting they're big, fat rabbits.

After Sister Jenkins leaves (still doubting Ras), Martha comes out to inspect the catch and finds the bag contains fresh-killed shoats.

"They're wild pigs," Ras pleads, but Martha knows better.

"I was just tryin' to put supper on the table," he says.

Inside, Martha tries to get Ras to pray with her, telling him they could be so much happier if he'd get religion. Ras agrees to try. Although he kneels down with Martha and she prays fervently (as the Choir sings "Were You There?") he is just uncomfortable.

While she goes back to her bed, Ras cleans his gun and then leaves it leaning against a chair. It slips to the floor and accidentally goes off, shooting into the next room and hitting Martha in the side. Ras runs to her, screaming, "Martha! Martha! Talk to me, honey! Oh, my goodness!"

Later, members of the congregation are gathered in the Jackson living room singing "Swing Low, Sweet Chariot" as they wait to hear of Martha's condition. In the bedroom, Ras finally is praying in earnest as he kneels at a chair beside her bed.

Privately, Sister Jenkins tells Sister Ellerby that Martha doesn't have a chance. The doctor has told her that the bullet went "clean through her" and came out to hit a picture of Jesus on the wall above the bed.

Ras joins in prayer with all the brethren as they ask Jesus to "drive the misery away" from Martha and also to drive the sin from Ras's heart so that he can "see the Light."

Ras goes back in to kneel by Martha's bed. Unseen by him, an angel comes to stand over Martha (to the singing of "I've Heard of A City Called Heaven"). The angel bids Martha's spirit to rise, and we see Martha's transparent form rise out of her unconscious body and follow the angel.

In a graveyard, the angel shows Martha the restless souls who are wandering around there near their graves, mourning "because their efforts are yet unrewarded, because the unjust have struck down the good and the unselfish, because sin is enthroned in the seat of power."

While the angel speaks, Martha also sees some unusual scenes which literally interpret the story of Jacob's ladder (which Director Williams borrowed from French director Georges Melies' 1916 film entitled *Going to Heaven*.)

When Martha asks why the angel has brought her here, the angel points her to a road—the Highway of Life—on which she must travel until she comes to a crossroads.

There, she must choose either the right fork, which leads to happiness and Eternal Life, or the left fork, which leads to death, Hell, and destruction.

"But walk clear of temptation," the angel warns her, "and beware of the hypocrite and the false prophet."

Martha finds herself alone on the country road in the daylight. Unbeknown to her, she is being watched by Satan and by his handsome earthly servant, Judas Green.

"Okay, Judas," Satan says, "go ahead—do your stuff!"

Approaching Martha as she is looking across the fields to a big city, Judas flatters her and offers her a silk dress, with shoes to match, which he tells her she will need in the city.

Not heeding the voice of the angel, who tells her that "Life is a more wonderful gift than clothing for the body," Martha accepts the clothes. Immediately, she is with Judas in a honky-tonk. They are both enjoying their drinks and the floor show, which is Bernice Gay's "acrobatic dance" and Gussie Smith's rendition of "Weary Blues." Martha is now in the middle of the city, with its dancing, drinking, and tempting high-life.

Judas introduces Martha to Mr. Rufus Brown, a "businessman" who says he can find her a good job, making plenty of money but with no hard work. Later, Martha finds herself upstairs in Mr. Brown's establishment and very nervous about what her "new job" is really supposed to be. When Brown comes to see what is keeping her, she tells him she has decided not to take the job. Angrily, he tells her she can't back out now—he has spent thirty dollars on those new clothes she is wearing and her first customers are already waiting for her downstairs. Weeping, Martha falls to her knees and prays for help. As she prays, the angel and Satan fight for her decision. Finally, Martha takes the angel's advice and flees from the roadhouse. When Brown and her would-be customers find her gone, they set out after her.

To the choral music of "Run, Child, Run," Martha runs down the chalky road and finally comes to the crossroads, chased by the angry men. She accidentally takes the left fork and runs into a group of jiving and drinking folk gathered around a jazz band on a flatbed truck—with Satan at the wheel, passing out whiskey. Realizing her mistake, Martha turns and runs the other way just as the men catch up with her.

"I ought to mash her brains out with this rock!" one of the men says.

But a Voice speaks to them, saying: "Stop! What has this woman done?"

"She stole my money, Lord!" one says.

"She ain't no good," says another.

"She's always robbing someone. She robbed me once!" Adds another, "She's a sinner!"

"He that is without sin among you," says the Voice, "let him cast the first stone at her!"

As they did thousands of years ago, the accusers slowly walk away. Struggling, Martha drags herself to the foot of a large, life-sized cross which is planted in the road. Angels gathered around the cross sing "Steal Away to Jesus." As Martha lies at the foot of the cross, drops of blood fall upon her forehead.

Back in bed at the Jackson house, Martha awakens and calls to Ras. At first, he cannot believe she is not a ghost, but she assures him that she is going to get well.

"But why did they stop singing?" she says, wondering, "I like to hear them sing."

Ras does not know what she is talking about, but he is ecstatic. He runs, calling to Sister Jenkins and the other "mourners," to tell them the good news and have them come witness his wife's miraculous recovery.

They all sing "Good News!" as they celebrate Sister Martha's return from the near-dead.

Dirty Gertie From Harlem, U.S.A.

CREDITS

Director: Spencer Williams
Producers: Alfred N. Sack & Bert Goldberg
Director of Photography: John L. Herman
Assistant Cameraman: Gordon Yoder
Original Story and Screen Adaptation: True T. Thompson*
Sound Engineer: Dick Byers
Properties: J. L. Bock
Art Director: Ted Solomon
Makeup: Frillia
Year of Release: 1946
Running Time: 60 minutes (5,378 ft.)

CAST

Gertie Larue: Francine Everette
Diamond Joe: Don Wilson
Stella Van Johnson: Kathrine Moore
Jonathan Christian: Alfred Hawkins
Ezra Crumm: David Boykin
Papa Bridges: L. E. Lewis
Mama Bridges: Inez Newell
Larry: Piano Frank
Al: John King
Big Boy: Shelly Ross
Tight Pants: Hugh Watson
Messenger: Don Gilbert
Old Hager: Spencer Williams
Specialties: July Jones (R. Orr), Howard Galloway, and
"6—Harlem Beauties—6"

*Plot is roughly adapted from Somerset Maugham's *Rain*

Diamond Joe joins the crowd in welcoming Gertie.

Mr. Christian (left) is outraged because Gertie's troupe has all the rooms.

Gertie meets Tight Pants and Big Boy.

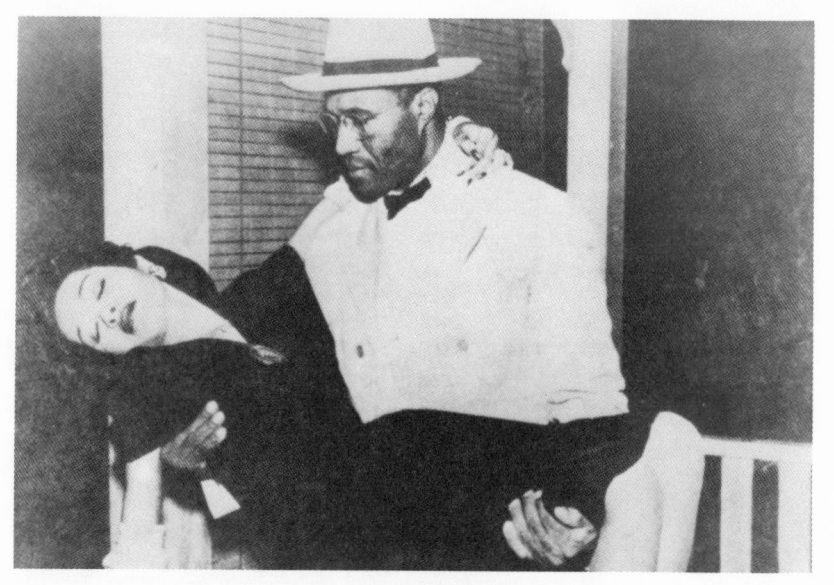

Mr. Christian carries the unconscious Gertie into the hotel.

Stella advises Gertie to see the voodoo woman, Old Hager.

Old Hager reads the crystal ball for Gertie.

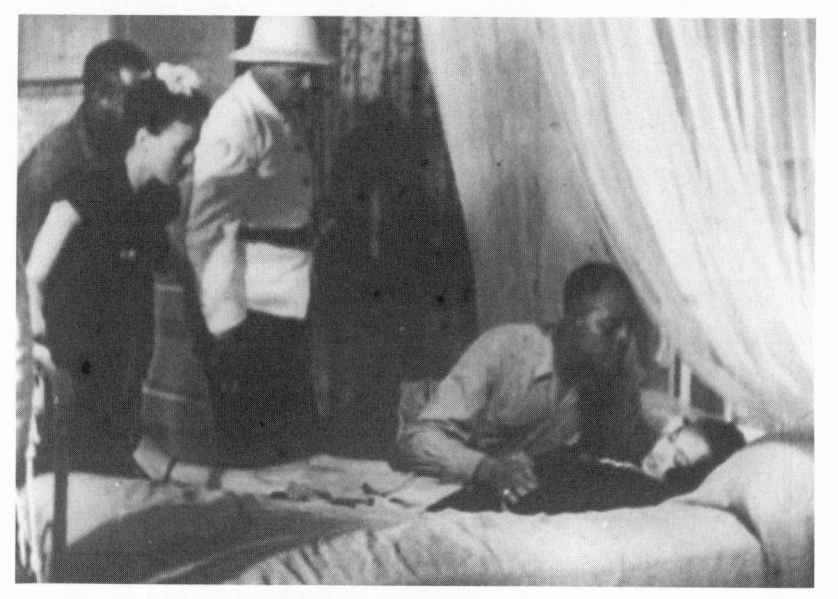

Gertie performs at the club.

"I killed her because I loved her."

Feverish preparations are going on at the Paradise Hotel. A banner on the hotel's front reads "Welcome Gertie." When a boat whistle sounds, the whole town rushes off to the docks and comes back escorting Gertie LaRue. Gertie is fresh from Harlem with her troupe of male and female dancers and singers. On a special grandstand built for the occasion, the local brass band plays "A Hot Time in the Old Town Tonight" and Papa Bridges, owner of the Paradise Hotel, formally welcomes Gertie to the island of Rinidad as "the greatest star that has ever hit this island."

As they are being checked into the hotel, Gertie reacquaints herself with an old friend, Diamond Joe, who owns the Diamond Palace where Gertie's show is to play. Diamond Joe tells Papa Bridges to give Gertie and her troupe the best rooms in the house. What impresses the newcomers most, however, is the heat and the mosquitos.

Stella, who is Gertie's self-appointed "watch dog," tells Gertie that she hopes Gertie can finally settle down a little and perhaps get something going with Diamond Joe, who obviously is going for her in a big way.

In their own dormitory-type room, the chorus girls have their own questions about Gertie. They wonder why she treated a Harlem fellow named Al so badly, especially when he had given her clothes, money, a car, and treated her like a lady.

"One of these days, she's gonna get what's coming to her," says one of the girls. They all agree that it's true.

Meanwhile downstairs, Mr. Christian and his assistant, Ezra Crumm, are trying to check into the hotel. Mr. Christian is outraged—first by the customs inspector having gone through his luggage and now by being told that there is only one room left in the hotel.

Instead of following the troupe manager's directions to get some rest, Gertie is restless. Against Stella's protests, she goes out, saying, "Nobody tells me what to do! I'm the star!"

"It's that kind of big 'I' and little 'U' that always gets you in trouble!" Stella shouts after her, adding that they'd all still be in Harlem if it hadn't been for the way Gertie "two-timed" Al.

Gertie does admit some remorse about her treatment of Al, but she brightens, saying, "When this thing blows over, it's 'Seventh Avenue and 135th St.—here we come!' Don't worry, honey, I'm through with all men!"

As Gertie passes through the lobby, Mr. Christian and Ezra are still having fits about their room assignments.

"You gave that show troupe the best rooms and we had to take what's left!" shouts Mr. Christian. "You gave us the worst rooms in the house!"

"If we're going to teach these people what sin is," Ezra adds, "we've got to be in more comfortable surroundings!"

"But Miss LaRue is a lady," protests Papa Bridges, "and naturally we favor her request."

"A lady?!" Mr. Christian splutters. "It's a wonder God doesn't strike you dead! She's a painted trollop! You should have seen her on the boat, carrying on with all those men. She's a Jezebel, I tell you!"

"Yes, Mr. Christian!" simpers Ezra, nodding obediently. "You're right, Mr. Christian!"

As Gertie passes, they exchange looks that could kill.

Outside, a sailor (Tight Pants) and a soldier (Big Boy) are looking at Gertie's poster and wishing they could meet her. Their wish comes true.

Over at the Diamond Palace, Diamond Joe is proudly showing Tom McAnn, the troupe's manager, all the facilities of his club. Joe admits he'd like to be in Harlem, himself, if it weren't for his big investment in the club. Seeing Gertie makes him realize what he's been missing all these years.

"But just between us, Joe," Tom tells him, "Gertie's hard to get and hard to hold. Give her half a chance and she'll run around on you. That's why they call her 'Dirty Gertie.'"

Diamond Joe warns the club's pianist, Larry, that Miss LaRue is a great star and he has to play her music on his piano like it's never been played before. When Larry sees Gertie's picture, he begins wondering where he has known her before—perhaps under another name.

Gertie brings Tight Pants and Big Boy into the club for a little drink. Joe sets up the drinks for them, then asks Gertie for a private conference in his office. On the way to the office, Joe introduces Gertie to the piano player, who looks at her very curiously. Gertie thinks maybe she's met him some place before, too.

In the privacy of his office, Diamond Joe gives Gertie a diamond necklace, saying, "I've waited for this moment for a long time—ever since I saw you doing your strip-tease in Harlem."

As Diamond Joe is confessing his love to Gertie, she hears a strange tune being played by the piano player. She is curious about him. Joe says he "drifted down here from Harlem a long time ago. He's nothing but a barfly, but he sure can play that piano." The tune haunts Gertie, taking her back to the old days.

Ezra sees Gertie drinking with the soldier and sailor at the Diamond Palace and rushes back to the hotel to tell the outrageous news to Mr. Christian. Furthermore, Ezra reports that there are posters of Gertie all over town, "and all she has on is a little teensy something. Everybody's looking at her!"

"I know my plan of battle clearly," Mr. Christian vows. "I'll go to this little woman and talk to her, reason with her. Then, if she does not listen, I'll go to the Governor and have him put her and her low-down cohorts off this island—send them bag and baggage back to Harlem!"

Later, Ezra comes down to the lobby looking for Mr. Christian, who is sitting there waiting for Gertie to come in. When Ezra tries to persuade him to go to bed, Mr. Christian refuses, saying that he must talk to this woman.

Finally, about four-thirty in the morning, Gertie and her crew drag in, loud and boisterous. Mr. Christian goes out on the veranda and sees Gertie having a last drink with the soldier and sailor. As Mr. Christian watches from hiding, she kisses both of the boys goodnight. After the boys leave, she thinks she sees the figure of Al, her old Harlem lover, lurking in the dark.

"Why don't you get out of my life and stay out!" she shouts at the figure.

As she goes to the hotel entrance, Mr. Christian comes out of the shadows and asks her to talk with him. Scared, she faints and falls into his arms. He takes her inside and lays her down on a couch, then brings her a glass of water. She regains consciousness to find him looking at her hungrily. She refuses the water he offers to her, as well as refusing his "instruction" about leading a more holy life.

"Take your hands off me, you dirty, psalm-singing polecat!" she shouts at him as he pats her on the shoulder in what he hopes is a fatherly manner. "If the truth were only known, you want me just like all the rest!"

"Have it your way, Miss LaRue," he says, drawing himself up, "but you haven't heard the last from me. The Lord moves in mysterious ways his wonders to perform!"

Back in her room, a shaken Gertie tells Stella about her encounter with Mr. Christian. Stella warns her that the man can make trouble for her—maybe even get her thrown off the island.

"And you can't return to Harlem," she adds: "Al's there, and he'd be sure to kill you!"

Gertie tells Stella about her feeling that she had seen Al earlier that night—only to have him disappear.

Stella advises Gertie to see the Voodoo woman the other girls are all talking about.

"They say she sure can tell you just what's gonna happen."

At the Diamond Palace, Diamond Joe walks in and finds his piano player asleep at his piano. He is talking in his sleep—to Al, saying that he has seen Gertie LaRue.

"I told you she was no good, Al," the piano player mumbles. "You should have listened to me. You should have killed her."

After he is finally awake, Diamond Joe asks him what that song is he was playing last night.

"It's a song a pal of mine wrote a long time ago, about a woman he was nuts about. She was a no-good rat."

Diamond Joe warns him not to play the song again because it makes Gertie upset.

In the hotel's restaurant, Mr. Christian and Ezra are eating. Mr. Christian looks very disturbed, not eating, and Ezra remarks that he is worried about him.

"This morning, I can see the path I must take quite clearly," the pensive Mr. Christian tells Ezra. "I'm going to the Governor and have him send this LaRue and her cheap rubbish off this island. They must not give their exhibition of filth tonight!"

Before going to see the Governor, Mr. Christian pays a visit to Diamond Joe at his night club, to see if he can be persuaded to cancel the show. Joe defies Christian, saying, "Just what are you gonna do about it?"

"That you will soon see," the outraged reformer spits.

During the rehearsal, Diamond Joe breaks in to tell the performers about Mr. Christian's threats and that they shouldn't worry, "because nothing and nobody will close this show! The show will go on!"

Diamond Joe tops this pronouncement by publicly giving Gertie another gift in keeping with his name—a diamond ring!

Just at that moment, the piano player forgets himself and plays the old song again. Hearing it, Gertie has a tantrum.

Back at the hotel, Ezra runs in to tell Mr. Christian that the troupe are going ahead with their show. Crestfallen, Christian says that his trip to see the Governor was to no avail—the Governor will not consider cancelling the show until he has seen it. Mr. Christian goes back to his room to ask the Lord's guidance. He explains to God how—if it is His will—he will slip into the Diamond Palace that night, "that I may be better able to judge in thy sight. Must I go? I'm listening. You want me to go? Yes! Thank you, Lord."

Down in the lobby, Mr. Christian and Gertie meet, but he turns away from her as she sashays up the stairs.

Later, Ezra is trying to convince Mr. Christian to let him see the show that night.

"If I don't see that show, I can't tell you what an awful, sinful thing it is."

"Heaven forbid! Don't even think of such a dreadful thought!" Mr. Christian warns him.

"I had a talk with the Lord," Mr. Christian says, "I can't reveal to you what he said to me—but don't you worry—I have his work to perform!"

Back in her room with Stella, Gertie is reveling in her new-found riches—"a diamond ring, a diamond necklace, a Sugar Daddy, a soldier, a sailor, and a preacher-man, if I wanta take the time to work on him. How'm I doing, Kid?"

"Better go easy," Stella warns her. "Some things don't look so good to me. I don't like the way that piano player looked at you. And there's that preacher-man—and another thing—I didn't like it when that black cat ran in front of us when we passed that alley. I'm not trying to scare you, but if it was me, I'd go see that old Voodoo woman real quick!"

Admitting that the black cat scared her, too, Gertie goes to see the Voodoo woman.

In a run-down house on the outskirts of town, Gertie meets the Voodoo woman, Old Hager (played by Spencer Williams himself).

"I want to know about my future," Gertie asks Old Hager.

After looking into the crystal ball until it begins to glow from within, Old Hager seems dismayed.

"It's better that you go home," the Voodoo woman tells her. "You should not know the truth."

When Gertie insists, Old Hager says, "I hate to tell you, but you've done something bad. I see a man. He's mad at you! Looks like he's coming after you. I see blood! That's bad."

At rehearsals, they're all wondering where Gertie is. She comes in late and, in her dressing room, tells Stella the Voodoo woman told her nothing but bad things and she thinks she was a fake. Just then, Gertie drops her mirror and it breaks.

"That's bad luck," Stella warns her.

That night is the big show. The opening act is a chorus line of the girls in evening gowns, with Gertie at their center. They are followed by July Jones and Howard Galloway, in white tie and tails, doing an excellent soft-shoe duet. Finally, in verse, July and Howard introduce Gertie, who goes into her strip-tease act.

Back in the darkness, we see Ezra. He is not so much interested in watching Gertie's act as he is in watching another shadowy figure hiding in the back of the club. It is Mr. Christian, who stands there, eyes glued to Gertie on the stage. He is obviously moved by many different kinds of emotions, much to the amusement of Ezra.

Before Gertie has done much more than get her gloves off, Mr. Christian rushes forward, shouting, "I command you to stop! Jesus threw the thieves out of the temple, and I shall do likewise!"

A general free-for-all ensues, and customers and showfolk scatter. Diamond Joe sees Gertie back to the hotel, warning her to "lay low until this thing blows over."

In her room, Gertie puts on her robe and grimaces at her reflection in the mirror.

"God! What a wreck!" she says of her reflection.

She puts a record on the old hand-cranked Victrola and goes out on the balcony for a smoke. "Blues in the Night" is the tune she is playing. The cigarette finished, she goes back in, cuts off the music and begins to perfume herself. Suddenly, we see a figure climbing up onto the balcony.

"I've come to get you, Gertie!" the man says as he enters her room.

"Al! I love you, Al. I've always loved you," she protests. "Let's go away someplace—any place—and start all over again! Kiss me, Al— kiss me!"

Instead of kissing her, Al shoots her—three times—then kneels down to embrace her body.

"I'll always love you," Al says.

Stella and the police rush in.

"Al, why did you do it?" Stella asks him.

"I killed her because I loved her," he answers.

The Girl in Room 20

CREDITS

Director: Spencer Williams
Producers: Jenkins & Bourgeois
Cinematographers: Frank Brodie & Jack Specht
Sound: Elmer Green
Editing: H. W. Kier
Music: "Be Sweet to Me," by Roger Cockrell
Year of Release: 1946
Running Time: 63 minutes (5,665 ft.)

CAST

Daisy Mae Walker: Geraldine Brock
Dunbar Hamilton: July Jones (R. Orr)
Mrs. Walker: Myra Hemmings
Jim Walker: John Hemmings
Mabel Walker: Margery Moore
Elviry Tatum: Mrs. F. D. Benson
Mamie Wilson: Mamie Fisher
Joe Phillips: Spencer Williams
Mr. Crowley: G. T. Sutton
Clementine: Katherine Moore
Duke Moody: E. Celise Allen
Arnold Richardson: Howard Galloway
Mrs. Richardson: Uncredited

SYNOPSIS

Talented Daisy Mae Walker is a young and ambitious girl who lives in Prairieville, Texas—a wide place in the road. She is singing her farewell song to her parents, her little sister Mabel and her boyfriend, Dunbar, before she leaves for New York City to seek her fame.

Dunbar sees Daisy Mae off to New York City.

The first friend she makes is Joe Phillips.

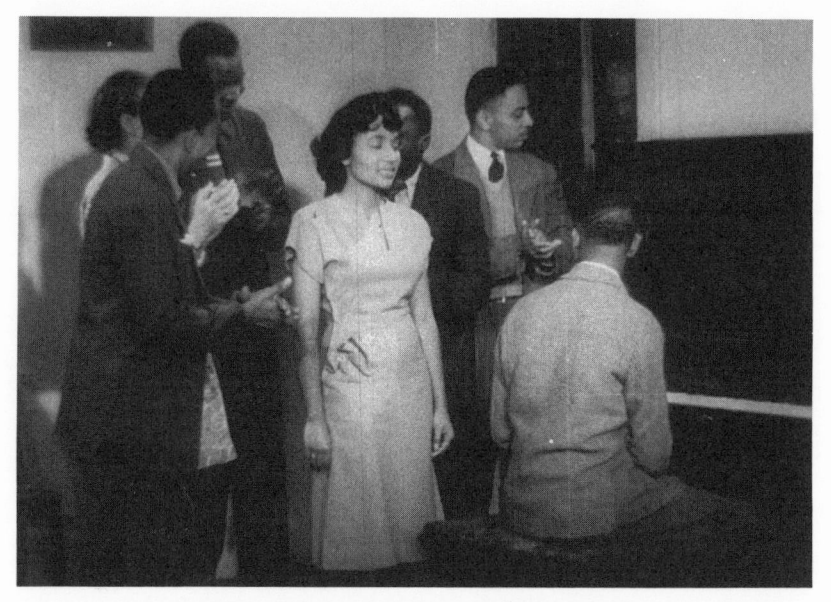

Daisy Mae auditions for a job with the band.

The family at home in Prairieville, Texas, worry about Daisy Mae.

Mr. Richardson makes advances toward Daisy Mae.

Mrs. Richardson shoots at her husband but hits Daisy Mae.

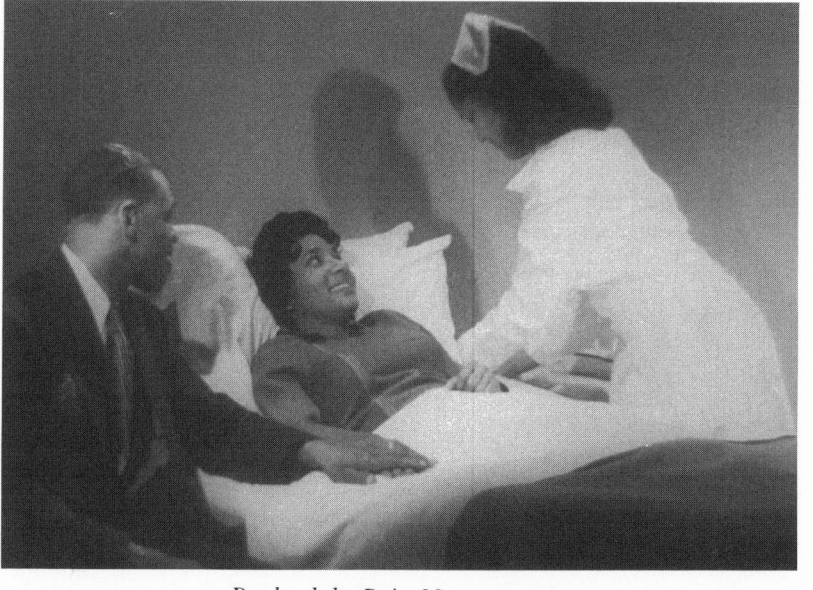

Dunbar helps Daisy Mae recuperate.

Finale at the Congo Club

With only forty minutes to catch the train, the family leaves Dunbar alone with Daisy Mae. Although he really wants her to stay and marry him, Dunbar does not protest against her going, but only tells her how much he loves her.

"I love you, too, Dunbar," she says. "After I've tried my luck in the city, I'll come back to you."

So, with eighteen dollars from her father, a sack lunch from her mother, and Dunbar's undying affection, Daisy Mae leaves, promising, "Some day I'll make you proud of me!"

After the train leaves, Dunbar goes back to his family's grocery store, where he is visited by Daisy Mae's voice teacher, Elviry Tatum. Elviry admits that she is the main person who urged the girl to follow her dream to New York City, and hopes that Dunbar is not mad at her for doing so.

"Look at the girls of our race who have risen to fame because of their musical ability," she tells him. "Marian Anderson, Dorothy Maynor, Etta Moten, Ella Fitzgerald, Lena Horne—and I'll bet they weren't all born in a big city, either. At least some of them must have come from small towns like Prairieville."

At Grand Central Station, Daisy Mae is looking for a cab and happens to find the one driven by Joe Phillips. He takes her to the address of her mother's old friend, a "Mrs. Jones." But when they get there, there is a sign outside saying "Mamie's Place," and he warns her not to go in there. She ignores his advice.

At the door, Daisy Mae is met by Mamie Wilson herself, who tells her that Mrs. Jones has moved to California, but invites her in for a drink, saying, "I could use a girl like you here."

Joe, who has waited to see what happens, gives a honk and Daisy Mae is able to use it as an excuse to make a hasty retreat.

"Any place you go will be better than the one you just left," Joe tells her. "Everybody in town knows Mamie Wilson—including the police!"

Joe takes Daisy Mae to an inexpensive but neat-looking hotel, where she is very much appreciated by a couple of men sitting in the lobby.

The men are members of a band. Their leader, Duke, comes to the lobby with the good news that their group is booked into the Congo Club the next week. He is also able to tell the hotel manager, Mr. Crowley, that their overdue rent will be forthcoming.

When Daisy Mae tries to pay Joe for the cab ride from Mamie's Place, he refuses, saying he has taken a personal interest in her because he has a daughter like her, and is even a grandfather.

As she waits for her room to be readied, Daisy Mae gets to know the two men from the band, and tells them that she's looking for a job so she can help her parents educate her little sister. She also tells them that she is a singer.

Upstairs in Duke's room, Clementine is cooking a meal on a hot plate, despite the big sign on the wall forbidding cooking in the rooms. At a knock on the door, they all begin feverishly hiding the hot food. But it is only the two guys from downstairs.

"Another free meal you looking for?" Clementine says disgustedly, hauling the hot plate out from under the bed. "Just let somebody open up a can of beans and up you pop like a Jack-in-the-box!"

Excitedly, the guys tell Duke that they just met a woman downstairs who looks like a million dollars—and she sings!

Duke decides a singer might be just what their band needs, so he invites her up to audition for them. They are impressed at her semi-operatic rendition of "Swing Low, Sweet Chariot."

A telegram delivered at that moment tells Duke that they are supposed to have a vocalist at their next gig, so he wants to hire Daisy Mae on the spot, with two weeks rehearsal before opening. She is flattered but a little scared at such quick success, and wants to think about it. Duke gives her until after the first rehearsal to decide.

At the rehearsal, Joe is watching and is worried about the attention shown to Daisy Mae by the club's manager, Arnold Richardson. Richardson invites the band to a party he is throwing that night at Mamie's Place, but they know the invitation is mainly for Daisy Mae.

At the party, Mr. Richardson is giving Daisy Mae a smooth line of talk.

"A talented, beautiful girl like you has to meet the right people, go the right places. You gotta show class! This club is no place for you," he says. He proposes to become her "agent," and will book her into really classy places. She protests that Duke and the band have been too nice to her for her to leave them, but says she will think it over.

As she leaves, she forgets her purse. Mamie is just going through the purse when Joe comes back to get it. She says he has no right to it and threatens to call the law. Joe takes the purse, warning her: "If you keep arranging for Richardson to meet these nice little country girls, you won't have to call the law—they'll be here!"

The next day, Joe finds Daisy Mae in the new apartment that Mr. Richardson has rented for her, "as her agent." He returns the purse to her, warning her that "anything over fifteen cents is cold meat for Mamie Wilson."

At home in Texas on the front porch, Dunbar and the family are waiting forlornly for Daisy Mae to write.

"Well, maybe she's too busy to write," Mrs. Walker says.

"Maybe she got married!" little Mabel pipes, much to Dunbar's distress.

Daisy Mae telephones Joe to come over and take a package to the post office for her. When he is helping her tie up the package, he misses his "frog-sticker" for cutting the twine, but Daisy Mae has one which she uses as a letter-opener. Along with the package, she gives him a letter she has forgotten to mail, and shows Joe the address of "Dunbar, my home-town boyfriend."

As soon as he leaves the apartment, Joe gets on long distance and calls up Dunbar.

"I think Daisy Mae needs to see you right away," he tells Dunbar. "I don't know, but I think she's in bad company. If you want to keep her that same, sweet little country girl she was—"

Dunbar is on the train to New York in a matter of minutes.

Duke and his band are right back where they started—no money and no gigs. But, they are glad Daisy Mae is doing so well for herself, with a swell apartment and new clothes.

"Yeah, but look what it's costing her," says Clementine cynically.

"Maybe that Richardson guy really is a right guy," says Duke hopefully. "Maybe he is trying to get Daisy Mae a break. After all, we don't know—"

"That ain't the way I heard it," Clementine retorts. "Everybody I meet on the streets tells me that Arnold Richardson ain't nothing but a wolf in sheep's clothing! And besides, he's got a wife—and living with her, too!"

Duke vows to go see Daisy Mae the next day to talk things over with her.

As if to prove Clementine's allegations, two women in a beauty parlor are talking about Daisy Mae and Richardson.

"He says he's her 'manager,' but if his wife ever finds out what he's managing," says one of the women, "it'll be too bad for him, and her, too."

The beautician is trying madly to "shush" the women, pointing to the lady in her chair. It is Mrs. Richardson!

Daisy Mae receives a visit from Mr. Richardson.

Meanwhile, Dunbar has gotten into town and is now riding in Joe's taxi to see Daisy Mae.

In the apartment, Daisy Mae is finding that Mr. Richardson is more interested in funny business than in real business. She resists his amorous advances.

As the cab drives up and Dunbar and Joe rush into the apartment building, they can hear Daisy Mae yelling: "Please, Mr. Richardson, not that!"

"Oh, yes, you will," Richardson is shouting, "I spent a lot of money on you, and time, too! What do you think I did it for?"

Dunbar breaks down the door and goes for Richardson. Joe enjoys watching the pretty evenly-matched fight until he sees Richardson's hand reaching for Daisy Mae's sharp letter-opener on the floor. His foot on Richardson's hand stops that.

The fight is about over when the door opens and we see Mrs. Richardson. She shoots at her husband, but hits Daisy Mae instead.

At the hotel, the band hears the bad news. They take up a collection among themselves, giving all they have to a fund to care for her at Charity Hospital. They keep up an all-night vigil in their room, singing "God Will Take Care of You" and waiting for news from the hospital. Finally, Duke rushes in.

"Well, gang," he says breathlessly, "I've got good news! Daisy Mae will be as good as new within ten days. Our prayers have been answered!"

They realize that in order to help pay Daisy Mae's hospital bills they will need a new job, but they need Daisy Mae's singing in order to get a job.

When hospital visiting hours are over, Joe brings Dunbar to the hotel to meet Daisy Mae's friends, and to get Dunbar a room. When Dunbar meets the band, he finds that he is a hero after the well-deserved beating he gave Richardson.

Fresh out of the hospital, Daisy Mae is given a homecoming party by the band. As she sits in a wheelchair, she sings Dunbar's favorite song, "Be Sweet to Me." As she finishes, another telegram comes for Duke. They have another booking at the Congo Club if they can bring Daisy Mae along.

But, as Duke tells Dunbar, there is a definite problem. In order to accept the job, the band will need new arrangements and new costumes—at a cost of about $500, which they do not have.

Knowing that Daisy Mae wants to sing again, Dunbar tells Duke, "I've got about $500 back home in the bank. I'll loan it to you."

As they are rehearsing at the Congo Club, the new manager is very impressed with Daisy Mae's singing.

"Wonderful! Splendid!" he rhapsodizes. "Seven nights a week, like sardines! This show has everything!"

But now, it is Dunbar's turn to get a telegram.

"You mean, it did have everything," Dunbar says, reading the telegram.

"You know," he says, "I think New York is a little too big for Texas folks like Daisy Mae and me. You see, they just struck oil on my ranch down there. So, I'm gonna take Daisy Mae back as my wife, and I'm inviting the whole gang to go down with us, and stay for as long as they like. What do you think, gang?"

Unanimously, they think it is a great idea.

Juke Joint

Director: Spencer Williams
Producer: Alfred Sack
Cinematographer: George Sanderson
Screenwriter: Spencer Williams
Original Story: True T. Thompson
Technical Advisor: True T. Thompson
Music: Red Calhoun and His Orchestra
Year of Release: 1947
Running Time: 60 minutes (5,378 ft.)

CAST

Bad News Johnson: Spencer Williams
July Jones: R. Orr
"Mama Lou" Holiday: Inez Newell
"Papa Sam" Holiday: Leonard Duncan
Honeydew Holiday: Melody Duncan
Florida Holiday: Katherine Moore
Jefferson Lee: Tilford Patterson
"Highlife" Harris: Albert Smith
"Juke Joint" Johnny: Howard Galloway
Bartender: Clifford Beamon
Waitress: Frances McHugh
Master of Ceremonies: Don Gilbert
Specialties by: Mac and Ace, Kit and Kat, The Jitterbug Johnnies,
and Duncan's Beauty Show Girls

Green and Vanderbilt plot their future.

A pool game at the Juke Joint

Dancing at the Juke Joint

Honeydew celebrates her victory in the beauty contest as Green and Vanderbilt look on in concern.

They are also worried about Florida going to Chicago with Juke Joint Johnny.

Mama Lou catches Papa Sam in the Juke Joint.

Mama Lou makes sure Florida will stay at home.

A Juke Joint lobby card

Dusty and hungry, Bad News Johnson and July Jones (later to suffer a name-change in the film) arrive by truck-bed in The Great Southwest—South Dallas.

"We are now following the advice of one of the finest men in American history," Johnson orates to Jones, "Mr. Horace Greely, who said, 'Go west, young man, and do your best; then come back east and spend your grease.' "

"Say, News," Jones counters, "how come I couldn't go back east and get my grease, then come down South and shut my mouth?"

Although they are down to their last 25-cent piece ("the last button on Gabriel's coat"), they need a place to room and board, so they have to think of a strategy. Jones approaches a young man in front of a store, spends the last quarter grandly on an astrology magazine and asks where they might find accomodations. The young man, who introduces himself as "Jefferson Lee," directs the gentlemen to his girlfriend's house, where a Mrs. Holiday may be willing to take them as boarders.

At the Holiday house, Papa Sam is asleep on the porch, dreaming of his soldiering days in World War I. Mama Lou disturbs his reverie with a straight pin.

"All you ever do is dream!" she berates him. "Samuel Holiday! That name fits you to a tee—you've been on a holiday ever since the eleventh day of November, 1918. If you don't get outta here and get a job, I'm gonna give you back your rib and get me another Adam before it's too late!"

She gives him a dollar to go to the butchers and buy some meat for dinner.

Inside, Honeydew is trying on her beauty contest gown. Mama Lou fawns over her, comparing her intelligence and good taste with that of her sister Florida, who only thinks about "men, men, and more men, instead of the higher things."

Mama Lou goes to answer a knock on the front door and finds Johnson and Jones. She assumes they are salesmen.

"No, no, dear madame," Johnson says grandly, "we are gentlemen of the first order!"

He introduces himself as "Mr. Vanderbilt Whitney," and Jones as "Mr. Green."

She is doubtful about taking in boarders, although she has a spare room. She says she will ask Jefferson Lee what he thinks about it when he comes this evening to take her daughter to the theater.

At the mention of the word "theater," Johnson gets his inspiration. He tells Mama Lou that both he and Jones are "not actors—the word is a vulgar name—but thespians!"

Mama Lou is impressed. She offers to give the theatrical gentlemen free room and board if they will consent to give her Honeydew some lessons about how to behave on the stage tonight.

"Mrs. Holiday, the gods of luck have frowned most favorably upon you," Johnson says, swelling. "Watch this—"

He goes into his own rendition of Shakespeare's *Julius Caesar*, then follows rapidly with a bit from *Romeo and Juliet*, which winds up with him kissing Jones' hand—much to the latter's amazed disgust.

"If you could only show my daughter how to act like that," Mama Lou says, "I could offer you and Mr. Jones free room and board for as long as you want it!"

Needless to say, they accept, and retire upstairs to rest before supper.

Instead of going to the butcher shop, Papa Sam has gone to Johnny's Juke Joint and is playing poker with his young friend, Highlife. When he gets "busted out" by a hand that he calls "really contributary," he heads for home and his punishment. He leaves behind his daughter, Florida, who is enjoying the flattery of Johnny, owner of the establishment.

Johnny offers to take Florida to Chicago that night, because "a beautiful girl like you ain't got no business going to seed in a town like this—you're too pretty!"

While Florida thinks over his offer, Johnny is called to the telephone. He tells his wife that he may be "a little late tonight, on account of business."

At the Holiday home, Mama Lou wonders what is keeping Sam and Florida, "two chips from the same block." But she comforts herself with the amazing good fortune of getting two theatrical gentlemen to tutor Honeydew into a winning performance.

Upstairs, "Mr. Green" wonders why they had to change their names.

"Hollywood is a big place, and folks from there have to have big names," "Mr. Whitney" tells him.

"But suppose we meet somebody here from Memphis?"

"In that case, you're just plain old July Jones and I'm Bad News Johnson—and maybe in jail if whoever we meet's a policeman!"

Unsatisfied at the explanation, Jones wonders why Johnson gave himself such a big-sounding name but gave him the name "Green?"

"It was all I could think of at the time," Johnson admits, but he has left the first name for Jones to pick.

"Only thing I know goes good with greens is cornbread," Jones says.

"Cornbread Green! That's a good name for the stage—like 'Butter-beans and Susie' or 'Spareribs and Hambone,'" Johnson assures him.

Downstairs, Papa Sam is trying to sneak in without the meat or the dollar. When he is captured by Mama Lou, he tells her a sobbing story about meeting a poor old widow lady with little starving children and no money to buy something to eat. After he gave her the money, she went to stand on the railroad track. The train was coming, but the old lady didn't move. It was coming closer, but the old lady didn't move. Then, finally, the train ran right into her.

"Then what?" Mama Lou asks.

"The poor old lady moved!" Sam answers.

It's too much. Mama Lou starts throwing everything in the kitchen at Papa Sam, until Honeydew intervenes.

Hearing the racket, Johnson and Jones just hope that it does not mean that supper will be late. Jones hopes it will be pork. Johnson tells him the Bible says people should not eat any animal with a split hoof.

"But I was weaned on pork!" Jones insists.

Johnson looks closely at him.

"The Bible was right!" Johnson says.

Honeydew is sent for supper meat so the guests upstairs can have a proper meal before going to the theater.

Around the table before dinner, Mama Lou warns her family to be on their best behavior that night. When Johnson and Jones come down to take their seats, Mama Lou asks Jones if he will "give thanks."

"Thank you, lady," Jones promptly replies. "And if we able, we gonna eat everything that's on this table. And if there's any left in the pot, bring it now while it's good and hot."

Johnson saves the day by intoning a proper blessing, then everyone at the table says a Bible verse. Florida chooses the briefest verse in the Bible, "Jesus wept," and little Melody prays, "I thank the Lord for this meal—and for some more meal!"

"Amen!" is Jones' heartfelt response.

After dinner, "Vanderbilt Whitney" is showing Honeydew how to walk by the numbers while "Cornbread Green" is nodding off by the same numbers. Finally, they announce that Honeydew is fully trained and ready for the beauty contest. Johnson and Jones retire to their rooms "to change."

"Why'd you tell them we was gonna change?" Jones asks upstairs, "when the only thing you can change is a pair of socks, and you can't do that but once? If you could button up that coat you got on, your trunk would be completely locked!"

Jones turns philosopher momentarily as he gives Johnson his wisdom that "a man's got two eyes, two ears, two hands, and two feet, but only one mouth—which means that he should see, hear, work, and walk twice as much as he talks."

Ready to go, Papa Sam asks Mama Lou how he looks in his suit.

"Like a bale of hay with the middle band busted off," she tells him.

Although Mama Lou warns Florida to finish the dishes and not leave the house as the rest of them leave for the theater, Florida is immediately on the telephone to Johnny, telling him she has decided to take him up on that offer of a trip to Chicago.

There is a full house in the theater for the beauty contest. The master of ceremonies has the girls come onstage, then holds his hand over each one's head, letting the audience applause determine the winner. First prize goes to Honeydew Holiday, "the rage tomorrow and choice of Hollywood and Broadway!"

Backstage, Papa Sam and Highlife congratulate Honeydew as Mama Lou and the others hurry home to prepare the lemonade and cake for the celebration. Highlife insists that lemonade is too weak for a girl who just won a beauty contest, and that they should take her to the Juke Joint for a proper celebration. Papa Sam is too weak to refuse.

As they enter the Juke Joint, the jukebox is playing and the jitterbugs are dancing. Papa Sam makes eyes at the waitress, who ogles him back. None of them see Florida, who is there with Johnny, packed bag and all.

At home, Mama Lou is worried at the delay. Johnson and Jones volunteer to go find them.

Back at the Juke Joint, Papa Sam has wandered off to find that waitress, while Florida asks Johnny to keep Honeydew and Highlife distracted so she can sneak into the ladies' room to change for the train. It is at this moment when Johnson and Jones arrive, spotting Florida. They tell Honeydew she had better go in there and get Florida out so they can all get back to Mama Lou's party.

Florida proudly tells Honeydew that she is done with this kind of life forever and is going to Chicago with Johnny. Honeydew gets on the telephone and calls Mama Lou, who tells her to keep everyone just where they are—she is coming.

Mama Lou dashes through the front doors of the Juke Joint, waving her umbrella like a sword. When Florida sassily tells her mother that she is going to Chicago "and can't nobody stop me!" Mama Lou starts beating on Johnny and Highlife with her umbrella. The audience loves the floor show!

As Mama Lou leads them all outside, she spots Papa Sam on a bench with the waitress, smooching. She swats them so hard with her umbrella that the bench overturns.

At home finally, Florida is screeching and screaming that she will not stay there.

"You will stay here!" Mama Lou promises her. "When I get through with you, you won't be able to sit down for six months!"

She takes Florida into the bedroom. Soon, we hear Florida howling from within. Jones goes to look through the keyhole.

"Hey, boy," Johnson remonstrates with him, "don't you know the Good Book says 'He that looks will go blind?'"

"Yeah," Jones says, "but for something like this, I can afford to trust one eye!"

This sounds right to Johnson, so he joins Jones at the keyhole.

Marching On

(re-release title: Where's My Man Tonight?)

CREDITS

Director: Spencer Williams
Producer: Alfred Sack
Cinematographer: Clark Ramsey
Sound: H. W. Kier
Screenwriter: Spencer Williams
Year of Release: 1943
Running Time: 83 Minutes (7,516 ft.)

CAST

Rodney Tucker, Jr.: Hugh Martin
Grandpa Tucker: George T. Sutton
Mama Tucker: Myra J. Hemmings
Martha Adams: Georgia Kelly
Rufus: L. K. Smith
Jenny: Clarissa Deary
Sergeant Keen: Emmett Jackson
Wash: "Pepper" Neely
Wimpy: Estrica McZekkashing
Hobo (Rodney Tucker, Sr.): J. W. Hemmings

(Note: It is probable that the original running-time of this film, as directed by Spencer Williams, was approximately 63 minutes. However, Jenkins and Bourgeois, a distribution company in Dallas, apparently made a new version of the film, re-titled *Where's My Man Tonight?*, to which they added twenty minutes of orchestra and dance performance—uncredited except for the subscript "featuring the Brownskin Models"—boosting the total running time to 83 minutes, which was a more marketable feature length in the 1950s. It was this later version—and title—which was found in the Tyler, Texas, warehouse.)

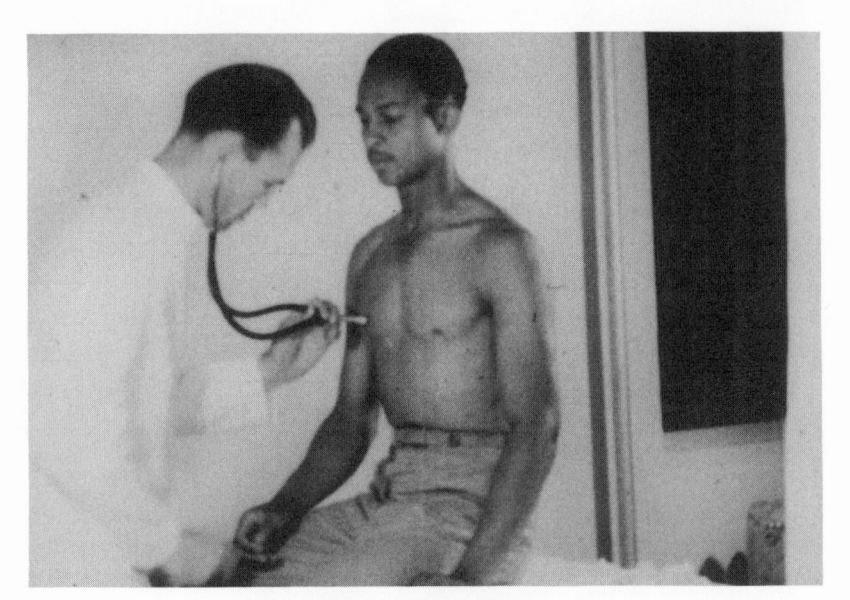

Rodney gets his physical.

Rodney at Fort Watchuga (filmed at the actual army base)

More K.P.

Rodney training

Grandpa Tucker (left) prepares to visit Rodney.

Rodney listens to his dying father.

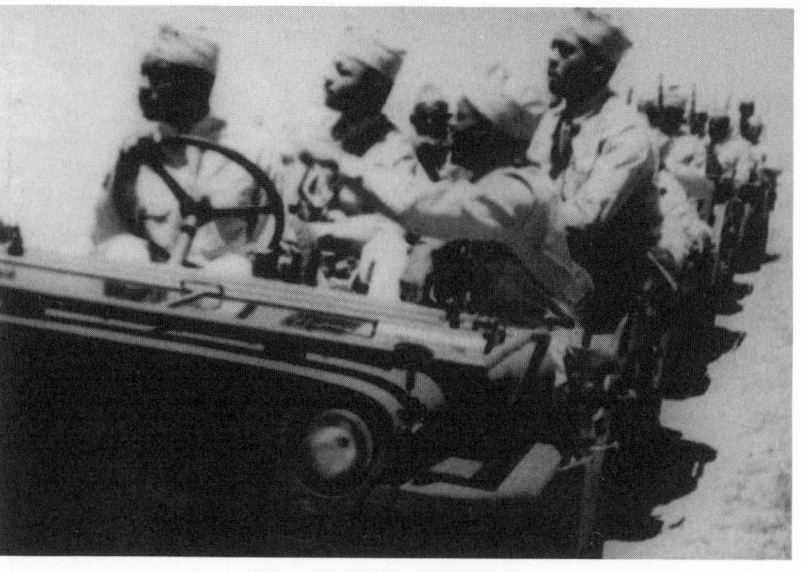

Rodney's unit comes to the rescue.

Happy Ending

In the early days of World War II, young Rodney Tucker, Jr., feels that he is being pressured by his family to volunteer for the army, which is something for which he has no great enthusiasm. His grandfather still wears his old Spanish-American War uniform and argues old battles with his crony, Rufus, and even Rodney's mother keeps on reminding him of what a good soldier his father, who never returned from World War I, was.

On the radio, Rodney hears that his girlfriend, Martha Adams, will be singing on stage as part of an Army recruiting rally in the town square that night. At the rally, he watches from the fringe of the onlookers as recruiter Sergeant Keen introduces Martha's song, then gives his pitch to "those men among you who are able-bodied." After the rally, Rodney meets Martha, who is not pleased to see him.

"You ought to be ashamed of yourself!" she berates him. "While other people are working their heads off to help our country, you sit back and enjoy yourself—and then you have the nerve to come here!"

When Rodney tries to defend his right to do as he pleases, Martha says, "You speak to me of marriage, but you haven't proven to be anything but a bragging coward!"

Their unhappy tête-à-tête is ended as she slaps him, throws their engagement ring on the ground and walks away.

For the next day or so, Rodney walks around town, trying to forget his troubles. But it seems that everywhere he goes he is reminded of the war by patriotic citizens. His indecision is ended as the mailman brings a letter to the Tucker house telling him that he has been drafted.

After Rodney has gone to be inducted into the Army, the family reads a letter from him. Grandpa is sorry that he ever doubted Rodney's patriotism. They are all now very proud of him.

The scene shifts to Rodney's training camp, Fort Watchuga in Arizona. (Obviously, Williams was able to get the Army's permission to film on a real, working Army base and to use regular soldiers as background extras.) In the barracks bull sessions, it is obvious that Rodney still does not take this war very seriously, refusing to believe that a strong country like the U.S.A. is in any real danger.

"That's a lot of hogwash (about the war situation being perilous to the U.S.). Let them (the European countries) do their own fighting," Rodney protests.

"This is just as much our country as it is anybody else's," Wash reminds Rodney.

"Well, even so," Rodney says, "what are we fighting for? We've got everything we need in this country. All the money, airplanes—everything. Now, I ask you gentlemen: what have we got to worry about?"

"Them Japs," answers Wimpy.

On his first full day at Fort Watchuga, Rodney gets in trouble for being the only man in his barracks to ignore reveille by sleeping in. As punishment, he is put on kitchen police duty for ten days. He fares no better on the drill field or on the rifle range. "You can do better than that, Tucker!" is the constant refrain of the sergeants and corporals.

Out in the field, a grizzled old sergeant is explaining the workings of a howitzer to Rodney and his fellow recruits. While the others move away to listen to another lecture, Rodney remains with the field piece to examine it further. He accidentally pulls the firing lanyard and it goes off, the explosive shell narrowly missing some other troops downfield.

More K.P.

At home in Texas, Grandpa Tucker is packing his old Model T to make a trip to see Rodney. He is taking all his old war souvenirs with the idea that he can make a display of them at Rodney's camp when he gets there "so them youngsters will have something to guide on!"

Hard at work washing dirty pots and pans, Rodney complains to Sergeant Keene that, although he has won the wrestling match and even the track meet for his company, he is treated like this. Sergeant Keen has even taken his girlfriend away from him! In answer, Keen invites Rodney over to his quarters that night for "a big surprise."

When Rodney gets to Sergeant Keen's room, he is surprised to find that Martha Adams is on the radio, doing a show from "a colored Army camp in Texas," but he becomes furious when she dedicates her song to Keen. Rodney takes a swing at Keen just as a superior officer comes into the room. Even though Keen says it was "just a misunderstanding," Rodney is confined to his quarters.

Back in the barracks, Wash and Wimpy try to cheer Rodney up by telling him that Miss Adams is coming to their camp the next day and wants to see him.

"This is all Sergeant Keen's idea!" Rodney explodes. "He deliberately planned that fight so he'd have me here when Martha arrives!"

Determinedly putting on his best uniform, Rodney tells them that he is going to break his restrictions and go to town so that he will not even be there the next day when Ms. Adams is in camp.

(This is where the 20-minute interlude takes place. It might be thought of as what Tucker sees in town that night as he goes on a drunken binge, from nightclub to nightclub—although there are no shots of him intercut into the performance footage.)

Rodney wakes up in a boxcar which is hurtling across the Arizona desert. His only companion is a hobo, who assumes that Rodney is on furlough and has chosen the boxcar as a cheap way to travel to his home. In their conversation, the hobo admits that he sleeps very little, because he has a tendency to walk in his sleep and he is afraid of walking right out of the boxcar while it is moving.

Rodney falls asleep again, and wakes up in time to see the hobo, in his sleep, about to walk out the open door of the speeding boxcar. Too late to stop him, Rodney jumps out to help. The old man is badly injured and delirious. He thinks that Rodney is his doctor, and keeps talking about "getting home to Ellen and the baby."

"Ellen?" says Rodney, at the mention of his mother's name. "Ellen who?"

At Rodney's urging, the hobo tells him her name is "Ellen Tucker," and that the baby was named after him—"Rodney Tucker, Jr."

As Rodney holds him, the dying old man's last words are, "I've got to go home! All soldiers go home now—the war is over! I've got to go home to Ellen—to my wife and baby!"

Rodney finally realizes why his father never came home from World War I—he has been in a hospital with amnesia all this time!

After burying his father, Rodney wanders in the desert, getting more and more tired and thirsty. First, he has visions of water—of waterfalls. But then, his visions change to those of a war which engulfs his home, injuring his mother and Grandpa Tucker.

Meanwhile, on the highway, Grandpa Tucker is stopped by a patrolman who asks if Grandpa has seen any sign of "three Japs." Feisty old Grandpa says that if he'd seen a whole regiment of Japs, he'd have shot them all.

Rodney is still wandering in the wasteland, about to die of thirst, when Grandpa happens to find him. It seems that Grandpa had seen some buzzards circling around off the highway and wanted to see what they were so interested in. He gives Rodney some water and takes him back to the car as Rodney tells of the miracle of finding, then losing, his father.

Somehow, the visions Rodney has had of war destroying his home and loved ones has convinced him that, if they'll give him another chance, he wants to go back to the Army and prove himself to be a man.

Back at the barracks, Wimpy is reading the local newspaper, and spots an article about a local "ham" radio operator who was able to pick up a Japanese-language broadcast on his one-tube set. The paper says that this means that the broadcast was probably made from nearby, and that it may have been made by spies.

Down in an abandoned mineshaft not far from where Rodney and Grandpa are, we see two Japanese civilians with a small radio set. The Japanese with the headphones smiles and hisses: "Aaaah! Banzai! We are to notify Operative Number Seventeen to carry out instructions to destroy objective number twenty-two. While stupid Americans are listening tonight on the radio to a message from their President, we will be listening to a message from the Mikado!"

Grandpa Tucker's old car has radiator trouble and the canteen is dry, so he and Rodney have stopped on the road to find a spring. Grandpa knows this country.

"Right up there is the entrance to Old Geronimo's Stronghold," he tells Rodney, "and halfway up that trail is a spring of water."

As they climb up, they notice the mineshaft. They are about to pass by it when Rodney finds a piece of paper on the ground with the words "Made in Japan." Thinking that this may have something to do with the spies Grandpa has told him about, Rodney goes down into the shaft to investigate. Not to be outdone, Grandpa follows.

When Grandpa and Rodney come face-to-face with the two Japanese spies, there is a great fight in which Grandpa is grievously wounded. Rodney chases one Japanese to the surface to keep him from getting away. As they are struggling, who should come by at the head of a column of jeeps and army men but Sergeant Keen! He sees the fight up on the hill and it is the Army to the rescue. They arrive in time to help Rodney subdue both the spies, but too late to save Grandpa Tucker.

"That's all right, son," Grandpa says. "It's just the way I wanted to die. The Lord has been good to me, letting me have one, last fight for my country."

Back at the Camp, Wash and Wimpy are worried about Rodney's trial for going AWOL (Absent Without Leave). Wash says that he could be shot for desertion in time of war.

Rodney enters grimly. Wash and Wimpy assume it is bad news, but Rodney says, "They gave me another chance to prove I'm an American, too! They're going to let me pay those scoundrels back for what they did at Pearl Harbor!"

As a reward for capturing the spies, Rodney is also going to be assigned to Grandpa Tucker's old regiment, the Fighting 25th U.S. Infantry.

Outside the barracks, Martha Adams has come over to congratulate Rodney personally for his bravery. She just happens to mention that she has joined the Womens' Army Corps, so they will be working together, it looks like.

"Do you still have that ring?" she asks coyly.

"Do you still have that finger?" he asks gruffly. They kiss.

Midnight Shadow

CREDITS

Director: George Randol
Producer: George Randol
Cinematographer: Arthur Reid
Sound: Carson Jowett
Editor: Robert Jahns
Production Manager: Wilfred Black
Assistant Director: Charles Hawkins
Music Director: Johnny Lang, with Lou Porter
Year of Release: 1939
Running Time: 54 minutes (4,833 ft.)

CAST

Margaret Wilson: Frances Redd
Lightfoot: Buck Woods
Junior Langley: Richard Bates
Mr. Wilson: Clinton Rosemond
Mrs. Wilson: Ollie Ann Robinson
Sergeant Ramsey: Jessie Lee Brooks
Buster: Edward Brandon
Prince Alihabad: John Criner
Mr. Mason: Pete Webster
Mrs. Langley: Ruby Dandridge
Mr. Langley: Napoleon Simpson

SYNOPSIS

There is an interesting prelude to this film, which reads:

"In the Southern part of this country lies a great land of romance and sunshine, known as 'The Old South.' Here, amid fertile fields,

Mr. and Mrs. Wilson want the best for Margaret.

Buster begs Margaret not to date Prince Alihabad.

A mysterious stranger watches through the window.

Prince Alihabad—the "smooth talker"

The killer strikes!

Lightfoot and Junior mistake the detective for the murderer.

Lightfoot and Junior at the stake-out

A happy ending

grassed areas of timber, oil lands and rippling rivers, live millions of black men and women in the most highly-concentrated area of Negro population in America. Here, in certain communities the like of which are found nowhere else in all the world, these people of darker hue have demonstrated their abilities in self-government by the orderly processes of law, of which they are capable when unhampered by outside influences. It is in a community such as one of these that the scene of our story is laid, and the events which follow are depicted."

After seeing many signs and posters announcing the coming attraction of "Prince Alihabad the Great: Mind Reader, Wonder Worker," we find the Prince himself in the living room of the Wilson family, with whom he is staying during his appearances in the city.

"I prefer to live in private homes, to get the rest and quiet which I need in my work," he tells his host as they visit before going on to the show. The Prince is to take young Margaret Wilson to the show with him, as his date.

Mr. Wilson asks the Prince about his "intentions" regarding Margaret. The Prince assures the old man that his intentions are honorable, but that he intends to earn sufficient money and to buy a little business of his own in a small town before he plans to settle down and marry. He had hoped that he and Margaret might reach "an understanding."

"We love our daughter very deeply," Mr. Wilson says. "Should she be made unhappy, I'm sure we could not stand it."

"Our little girl is all we have," agrees Mrs. Wilson. "Please don't go on with this make-believe, if that's what it is."

The Prince assures them that, although his family has always insisted that its sons marry into affluent circumstances, he is sure that they will understand, in this case.

Mr. Wilson is about to assure the Prince that his daughter will not be a pauper when the time comes for her to marry when Buster comes to call upon Margaret. Buster has been Margaret's boyfriend before the Prince came into town, and now he is furious but pessimistic about his chances. Quietly, Mrs. Wilson tells him to buck up and not let the Prince take her away.

Mr. Wilson goes to the strong-box in their bedroom and gets a deed and a map to show the Prince. It is to a piece of East Texas oil land which has been in their family for generations. Now, geologists have found that the famous East Texas oil structure runs right through it. They have been offered a lot of money for it already, but they plan to give it to their daughter and her new husband as a wedding present.

Mrs. Wilson frets because Mr. Wilson has shown the deed to the Prince.

"I just don't like to brag, that's all," she says.

Margaret finally makes her entrance, to find the frustrated Buster waiting for her. He insists that he will not let her go out with "that phoney" to the theater, of all places, but she is scornful of him. Defeated, Buster stalks out.

After the Prince and Margaret leave for the show, Mr. Wilson says that the Prince seems to be a fine young fellow.

"I guess so," Mrs. Wilson says uneasily, "but I have the queerest feeling that something's going to happen."

Meanwhile, in the comfortable and affluent Langley home, Junior Langley is working hard with his detective kit, learning how to lift fingerprints.

"Our boy works so hard, and you don't do a thing to help him!" protests Mrs. Langley. "You're always talking about what a good thing you have in politics, yet you do nothing for your own. Why don't you get him on one of those big cases?"

"I'm waiting for Mr. Hoover to get a case where he needs a fingerprint expert," Junior pipes up. "Then I could go to Washington!"

At home after the show, the Prince is giving Margaret his smooth "line," offering to take her to all the pretty places in the world as his wife.

"I'm just a small-town girl," she protests coyly. "You might be ashamed of me."

But the Prince insists that she must pack a few things so that they can elope very early in the morning.

Later that night, as Margaret is writing a sad refusal letter to the Prince to slip under his door, we see a strange shadow lurking around outside.

When the house is dark, the same figure slips into Mr. and Mrs. Wilson's bedroom and holds a vial of something under their noses. When Mr. Wilson continues to stir, the figure gives him another dose, then takes the strong-box from the dresser and leaves.

In the morning, Margaret awakens late and is puzzled to find no one stirring. She goes to her parents' bedroom and finds her mother unconscious and her father dead, strangled in the bedclothes. Near hysteria, she calls her friends, the Langleys, for help.

Mr. and Mrs. Langley rush out to help Margaret, telling Junior that they'll call him if there is anything he can do. After they have gone, Junior gets a call from his partner, "Detective Lightfoot," asking "Detective Langley" to come down and let him into the office because he can't find his key. As soon as he hangs up from that call, he receives another, from his distraught mother. She tells him about the disaster at the Wilson home and tells him to come as fast as he can—"they need an expert!"

When Junior and Lightfoot arrive at the Wilson home, the police are already there.

"Where have you been so long?" Mrs. Langley rebukes her son, "Hurry up! All the good clues will be gone before you get started!"

The two "detectives" go into the bedroom—the scene of the crime—to see what clues they can find. They find a strange man in there, so they subdue and handuff him, only to be full of apologies when he introduces himself as "Sergeant Ramsey of homicide."

Mr. Langley enters and tells the insulted Sergeant that the Chief of Police has said that, because the Wilsons were such good friends of the Langleys, Junior has the Chief's permission to work on the case.

"Yeah," says the Sergeant. "He'll be a lot of help!"

In the living room, the now-recovered Mrs. Wilson gives her recollection of the crime. There was a dark figure with a slouch hat and turned-up coat collar who entered their room, she thinks. She tried to wake up, but could not, and felt as if someone were smothering her with a pillow. When she finally did awaken, there was a strange taste in her mouth and she found her husband strangled in the bedclothes.

Buster does not have a very good alibi when he is questioned. He was so angry that he went for a walk to cool off, he tells the officers. His mother is no help.

"He didn't come home at all last night," she says, "but I know he didn't do anything wrong!"

Buster asks the Sergeant why they don't pull in "that Hindu who was here last night," and tells about Mr. Wilson showing the map and the deed to Prince Alihabad.

"He also told him an oil company down in Shreveport wanted to pay him a lot of money for the lease," Buster testifies.

"So, you sneaked in and took the deed to make it look like the Hindu took it," the Sergeant pours it on Buster. "Isn't that the way it was? You didn't mean to kill him, did you, Buster? You just wanted to keep him asleep long enough to sneak in and get the deed out of the drawer. You didn't know that Mr. Wilson had heart trouble, did you? You didn't know that when he started to resist and got tangled up in the sheets in spite of himself—you didn't know it would turn out that way, did you, Buster?"

The Sergeant decides to hold Buster as a suspect. To cover all possibilities, he sends out a general alarm to have the Prince picked up and brought back on charges of suspicion of murder. Then, he lets everyone else go so that he can compare notes with all the detectives on the case.

Junior and Lightfoot think maybe that means them, too, but they discover that neither of them has taken any notes so far.

"I was going to show him your notes," says Lightfoot. "I'd like to kinda keep mine secret. Here I been giving you the chance to get all the dope, and what do you get?"

"Well, now that's different," Junior says. "I didn't know this was a dope case. Who used it?"

The meeting of detectives is in the murder room, where the corpse is still on the bed. Junior thinks he will wait until they have removed the corpse before he goes in.

"Don't be so scared. That man can't hurt you," Lightfoot tells him.

"I know he can't hurt me," Junior protests, "but he can make me hurt myself!"

They get into the murder room before anyone else arrives, and decide to look for some more clues. With his magnifying glass, Junior can not find anything under the bed but cat prints.

"Coulda been one of them were-cats," he mumbles to himself.

Lightfoot, in order to re-enact the crime for himself, lies down on the bed—and falls asleep.

Under the bed, Junior gets tangled up with the cat, scaring Lightfoot so much that he gets tangled up with the sheets. They are trying to 'capture' each other when the Sergeant comes in and stops them disgustedly.

Junior has an idea. If he were the murderer and had the deed, there is just one place he would go—to that oil company in Shreveport that wanted to buy the land! They decide to go there and do a stake-out. To do the job right, Junior dons his Sherlock Holmes outfit, complete with pipe and deerstalker hat.

In Shreveport, they meet Mr. Mason, president of the oil company. Mr. Mason agrees with the fellows that it would be logical to expect the murderer there, so he calls the local police to alert them and promises to stay in touch with Junior and Lightfoot.

After three days of watching everyone in town, Junior and Lightfoot decide that no criminal with an ounce of brains would come to the one place he is expected, and that they should probably just go home right after they complete their surveillance of the stranger they have been following since that afternoon. Lightfoot is about to resign when they notice the stranger entering the oil company's building. They go to find a policeman.

In the oil company offices, Mr. Mason has just told the detective on stake-out that he can go home for the night when the stranger enters, unseen by the detective. He threatens Mr. Mason with a knife if he does not open the safe and give him money for the deed. (It turns out that the shadowy man is someone we have never really seen before.)

"The man I stole the deed from is dead," the stranger says, "and one more murder won't make much difference."

At that moment, the local detective enters and captures the stranger. His friend, the railroad detective, had told him that a strange character had gotten off a train from Oklahoma that day, and should be followed.

Junior and Lightfoot arrive after the suspect has already been cuffed.

"If you're sure them handcuffs are on tight," Junior tells the detective, "I'll arrest him again."

Back in Oxley, Sergeant Ramsey congratulates Mr. Langley on the fine detective work his son has done.

"Just a case of simple deduction, Sergeant," Mr. Langley says proudly. "That boy's gonna be a great detective some day!"

"He's a great detective now!" declares Mrs. Langley.

After Junior and Lightfoot arrive with the murderer and he is put in jail, the Sergeant frees Buster. But there is still the question of the Prince. Who is he? What is his right name?

The Prince refuses to say.

Finally, Buster hauls off and hits the Prince, flooring him. Apparently, Margaret thinks this was a very masterful thing for Buster to do, so she embraces him for a happy ending.

Miracle In Harlem

CREDITS

Director: Jack Kemp
Producer: Jack Goldberg
Cinematographer: Don Malkames
Editor: Don Drucker
Original Story & Screenplay: Vincent Valentini
Musical Director: Jack Shandlin
Specialty Numbers:
"I Want to Be Loved" by Savannah Churchill
"John Saw the Number" by Lavada Carter
"Patience & Fortitude" by Norma Shepherd
"Chocolate Candy Blues" by Juanita Hall
"Watch Out!" by the Lynn Proctor Trio
Year of Release: 1948
Running Time: 73 minutes (6,569 feet)

CAST

Aunt Hattie: Hilda Offley
Julie Weston: Sheila Guyse
Bert: William Greaves
Jim Marshall: Kenneth Freeman
Alice Adams: Sybil Lewis
Swifty: Stepin Fetchit
Minister: Creighton Thompson
Manley: Jack Carter
Mr. Marshall: Lawrence Criner
Detective: Al "Slick" Chester
and the Juanita Hall Choir

Aunt Hattie advises Julie and Bert.

Mr. Marshall decides to take over Aunt Hattie's candy factory.

Everyone is pleased with the new business arrangement.

Jim tells Alice that she is too old for him.

Police arrive to investigate Wilkinson's death.

A detective grills the suspects.

Julie becomes the chief suspect.

Aunt Hattie gets the candy business back.

SYNOPSIS

A Wednesday evening prayer meeting is being held in Aunt Hattie's spacious living room because she is too sick to attend regular services at the church building.

After the service, the Minister joins Aunt Hattie in her candy factory, which is part of her apartment. There, he sees Swifty, Aunt Hattie's deliveryman; Julie, her niece who helps her make the candy; and Bert, whom Aunt Hattie has raised like her own son since his parents died, and who is just home from the war.

Aunt Hattie declares that she is not long for this world, but that Julie is set to take over the candy business and Bert is studying for the ministry.

Julie wants to modernize and expand the candy factory, but Aunt Hattie is against it, just like she is against modernizing religion.

"People want to advance now, more than ever," Bert says, "and religion comes in for its share."

The talk turns to what Bert learned in the Army's Chemical Warfare Unit, that poison—just like change—is not dangerous unless you want it to be.

In a Harlem police station nearby, word comes on the teletype that Philip Manley, a confidence racketeer from Chicago, is probably in the Harlem area and is involved in a check swindle with the son of another candy manufacturer in town, Jim Marshall. Manley is wanted for questioning in a murder case, also.

Detectives go to the offices of Mr. Marshall, prosperous owner of a large candy factory, who tells them he has already settled the check matter personally, on behalf of his son. After the detectives leave, Manley tells his secretary, Alice, that he wants no more money sent to his son, he wants nothing more to do with the boy. Manley sent him to Chicago to study chemistry—so necessary to the workings of a candy-making factory—but he refused to study and only got into trouble with bad checks.

In another vein, he assures Alice that she has filled his life since his wife died and he will take good care of her in his will.

Back in Aunt Hattie's candy kitchen, Swifty is doing a complicated stacking and re-stacking of a dozen boxes of candy, trying his best to figure out the shortest distance he will have to walk "on these poor feets of mine" to deliver them.

Aunt Hattie reveals to Bert and Julie that she has had premonitions of her death, and that she has already ordered her casket and wants it brought to the apartment. She is thinking of having the Minister preach her funeral a little early, so she can see how it will go. Bert and Julie try to dissuade her, but she is adamant. Finally, Julie sings her to sleep with her favorite spiritual, "Look Down That Lonesome Road."

Mr. Marshall's errant son, Jim, shows up at the Marshall Candy Company's offices, breaking up a meeting between Mr. Marshall and his assistant, Mr. Wilkinson. They had been talking about how Aunt Hattie had turned down a very generous offer to buy out her business.

After Mr. Marshall tells Jim that he has cut off his allowance, that he will get no more until he goes to work, and that his bad behavior killed his mother, Jim angrily retorts that he is going to team up with Aunt Hattie and develop her business into some real competition for his father.

As Jim storms out of his father's office, he finds Manley waiting for him in the reception room. When Manley threatens to tell the old man about some more illegal matters in which his son was involved, Jim anxiously promises to get Manley some money if he will only keep quiet.

Back in Mr. Marshall's office, Alice says that Jim had a good idea. They should use Mr. Wilkinson as a "front," have him buy into Aunt Hattie's business as a partner, fix up the factory, then squeeze her out. Mr. Marshall thinks it is a great idea, and promises Wilkinson a nice bonus if he brings it off.

Everyone, including Aunt Hattie, seems pleased with Mr. Wilkinson's pledge to fix up the factory, enlarge it, and even get extra help if needed.

"Extra help! That's just what the doctor says we need for my bad feets!" says Swifty.

So the deal is signed, with Aunt Hattie getting 40% and Mr. Wilkinson 60% of the business.

When Jim hears about his father taking his idea away from him, double-crossing him with it, the father magnanimously offers to make Jim the manager of the operation.

Things are looking up in the candy kitchen. One of the new helpers,

(Juanita Hall), is singing "Chocolate Candy Blues" to the pleasantly-embarrassed Swifty. But it is obvious that Julie is going to have trouble from the amorous advances of Jim. When Bert catches Jim making a pass at Julie, there is almost a fight.

At Jim's apartment that night, Manley comes and threatens to involve Jim in a murder rap if he doesn't pay off soon. While Manley is there, there is another knock on the door. Manley hides as Alice enters. She tells Jim that it was her idea to send him to study with Manley in Chicago, but if he does not stay clear of Manley and his illegal doings now, it will be very hard for her to square it with his father. When she tries to remind Jim of an affair they had, he brushes her off, saying they were just good friends and she should have "known the score." She reminds him of all she has done for him, protecting him from his father and making sure the father did not cut Jim entirely out of his will, leaving everything to her.

"I'd hoped we'd be married," she tells him.

"Ridiculous!" Jim sneers at her. "You know you're too—"

"Too old for you, Jim?"

"Yeah, too old!"

When Alice leaves, Manley comes back in, having heard everything. He warns Jim that the old man will sign everything over to her in his will unless Jim stops him.

"You know something about poison, don't you?" Manley asks him slyly.

"Yeah," Jim answers, just as slyly. "I learned it from you!"

As Julie is closing up the kitchen for the night, Jim makes his play for her. She threatens to fire him if he does not quit making passes at her.

"That's funny!" he laughs. "Fire me? When my old man owns this place? I can take it over any time. But I won't, if you sorta make me— change my mind."

Jim tries to embrace her and there is a struggle which lasts until Bert comes dashing in and gives Jim a thrashing.

The next day, Mr. Wilkinson comes to Julie and says he has instructions from Mr. Marshall to close her out and take over the business. If she resists, he promises her, she will be sorry.

"Mr. Marshall is the one who'll be sorry," she sobs. "He'll never get away with this! He's the one who's gonna be sorry!"

Bert is just telling Aunt Hattie how she should get rid of Jim Marshall when Julie bursts in to tell them, "We've lost the place. It was all a trick. We've been swindled!"

In the Marshall Candy Company's executive offices, Mr. Marshall, Mr. Wilkinson, and Alice are celebrating the elimination of their company's number-one competition. But when Mr. Wilkinson asks for the bonus he was promised, Marshall refuses, calling his assistant "a weak sister" and telling him it was only pity that kept him on the payroll this long.

"I'll fix him!" Wilkinson tells Alice after Marshall leaves the office. "I'll show him I'm no weak sister!"

The undertakers are bringing Aunt Hattie's coffin into her living room, much to Swifty's dismay.

"Ain't nobody dead around here, is they?" Swifty asks, feeling himself up and down. "I feel all right!"

Back in his office again, Mr. Marshall tells Alice that he has just been to his lawyer and has left everything to her in his will. When she asks if Jim can break the will, he answers that he has left Jim the sum of one dollar and the will is iron-clad.

Alice brings Mr. Marshall a sample of his "latest conquest"—one of Aunt Hattie's chocolate drops. He eats one and, while admiring its unusual, rich flavor, he chokes and falls over dead.

The police detective pronounces that Mr. Marshall died instantaneously from a dose of arsenic in the candy.

Bert is still trying to get Aunt Hattie not to go on with her idea of her "early funeral," but it takes place anyway with Aunt Hattie sitting near her coffin and listening appreciatively to everything the Minister says about her. In the middle of the service, the police burst in to arrest Julie Wilson on suspicion of murder because Mr. Marshall was poisoned by candy that came from her kitchen.

At the police station, Alice and Jim and Mr. Wilkinson are all making the case worse and worse against Julie. Julie admits making the threat, but says she didn't mean she would kill him. She is paroled into the custody of the Minister. As they all leave, the detective says that any of them could have had a motive for killing Mr. Marshall.

Jim Marshall is throwing a lavish party at his apartment, complete with a singer and a trio. He brags to the girls that he is thinking of financing a new musical. He has also had Swifty bring in sample boxes of his New Orleans Chocolate Drops for all his guests. As he gets drunker, he tells his guests that Manley has been blackmailing him for years, but he is too smart for him now.

Meanwhile, the police have discovered a bottle of arsenic in the candy kitchen's medicine chest. To the detective, this means it looks like Julie is the guilty one. He sends his men out to pick her up and also to bring in Jim Marshall, who may know something about the poison in the medicine chest.

Manley manages to crash into Jim's apartment and threatens to tell the police all he knows about the poison, enough to pin a murder rap on Jim.

Jim rushes to his father's office to get the keys to the candy kitchen. At the office, he finds Alice going over the company books. He is shocked when she tells him that everything is going to her in the will.

At the candy kitchen, Jim is looking noisily through the medicine cabinet for the bottle of poison he has left there. Julie hears the noise and comes into the kitchen. She accuses him of being the murderer and they struggle. In the darkness, a third person comes in and knifes Jim.

As Julie screams, the lights suddenly come on and the police are there, seeing her standing over Jim's body.

"There's no doubt about it this time, Miss Weston!" they say.

In a jail cell, Julie tearfully tells the Minister that she can barely remember somebody coming in and grabbing the knife—to protect her, she thought at the time.

She is grilled unmercifully by the detectives, then put on the line-up. In the midst of the bright lights and the humiliation, she faints.

When Bert comes to see her, Julie wonders what she ever did to deserve all this trouble. Just because she wanted to expand the candy kitchen, they now have nothing left.

"Did you say 'nothing?' Darling, we've got everything! Yes, our love for each other!" Bert tells her.

Meanwhile, Aunt Hattie is hatching a plot with Swifty.

"Can you keep a secret without running all over the neighborhood telling it?" she asks him.

"Bad as my feet is, I couldn't even walk all over the neighborhood!" Swifty assures her.

She gives him a note for the detective. Nobody is to know he ever got it. Nobody.

"Not even me?" Swifty asks. "I'll hafta shut my eyes when I deliver it."

At the police station, the detective is so suspicious of Swifty's fumbling actions that he makes Swifty very nervous.

"What are you nervous about?" Swifty is asked.

"I ain't exactly nervous," he says. "I just generally falls to pieces around polices! Where the Law generally is, I ain't."

Swifty finally delivers the secret note to the detective, and is followed by Bert, who thinks the police should know that a man named "Manley" came to see Jim Marshall several times.

"Boys, we've got places to go!" the detective says excitedly to his assistants. "There's something I want Manley to hear, so let's get the old grapevine going!"

In a fast montage of faces, mouths talking, telephones and ears listening, we get the impression of a piece of news flashing around town quickly.

In Aunt Hattie's living room, she is lying in her coffin as if dead, clutching a fountain pen in her folded hands. A shadowy form comes into the room and tries to get the pen out of her hands. She rises up in the coffin and moans, "Vengeance is the Lord's! Thy brother's blood is upon thee!"

"Yes—I am the murderer!" confesses the man, whom we now see is Manley, "I killed Jim Marshall—and I'll kill you, too!"

But before Manley can harm her, the lights come on and the police jump on him, taking him away to be booked for the murder of Jim Marshall.

In the Marshall Candy Company's office, Alice is accusing Mr. Wilkinson of murdering both of the Marshalls when the police come in.

Alice tells the detective that Wilkinson is a 'lab man' and knows things like how a tiny capsule of poison can be inserted into a chocolate drop.

The detective brings Manley in. He tells them that the Chicago police have told him that Alice and Manley once had a love affair going.

"Yeah," says Manley, "and she double-crossed me for Jim Marshall!"

Manley tells of how she managed to have young Marshall go to Chicago where she told Manley to get him mixed up in some trouble in order to show Mr. Marshall that his son was worthless.

"But she didn't plan you leaving your fountain pen with your initials on it lying around near the murder, did she?" the detective asks. Then, he turns upon Alice.

"You knew all the poisons from Manley. You'd have no trouble fixing those candies," he accuses her. "A short time ago you mentioned the 'poison capsule'—well, no one but the police and the killer knew how that candy was poisoned!"

Backed into a corner, Alice confesses, "I wanted his son, Jim. It was the only way I could get him. Now he's gone—everything's gone!"

The detective stops her as she tries to swallow another of the poison capsules she had in her purse.

Back in the candy kitchen once more, Bert, Julie, Swifty, and the Minister are still worried about Aunt Hattie's pessimistic attitude. But Aunt Hattie comes walking in, out of her wheelchair, and says she's decided to get well. In one breath, she tells Swifty to get rid of that coffin and warns Bert that if he does not marry Julie before she gets into any more trouble, she will give him a spanking just like she used to.

"That's getting out of one trouble and right back into another," Swifty mumbles.

"But some troubles," says Aunt Hattie, smiling, "are worth-while!"

Murder In Harlem

(original title: Lem Hawkins' Confession)

CREDITS

Director: Oscar Micheaux
Producer: A. Burton Russell (Mrs. Micheaux)
Cinematographer: Charles Levine
Sound: Harry Belock and Armand Schettin
Screenwriter: Oscar Micheaux
Production Manager: Charles P. Nason
Art Director: Tony Continenta
Year of Release: 1935
Running Time: 98 minutes (8,794 ft.)

CAST

Henry Glory: Clarence Brooks
Claudia Vance: Dorothy Van Engle
Lem Hawkins: Alec Lovejoy
Mr. Brisbane: Andrew Bishop
Mrs. Epps: Laura Bowman
The Catbird: Bee Freeman
Mrs. Vance: Alice B. Russell
Detective: "Slick" Chester
Second Detective: Oscar Micheaux
Also: Lionel Monagas, Sandy Burns, Lea Morris, Joie Brown, Jr.,
Eunice Wilson, Henrietta Loveless, Lorenzo McClane, Helen
Lawrence, David Hanna, Byron Shore

SYNOPSIS

A black nightwatchman at the National Chemical Labs, on his midnight rounds, discovers the body of a young white woman in the plant's basement. He calls his boss, Mr. Brisbane, but is unable to reach him.

The nightwatchman describes how he found the body.

Henry Glory sells his book to Claudia and her mother.

Claudia and Henry fall in love.

Years later, Claudia hires Henry to defend her brother.

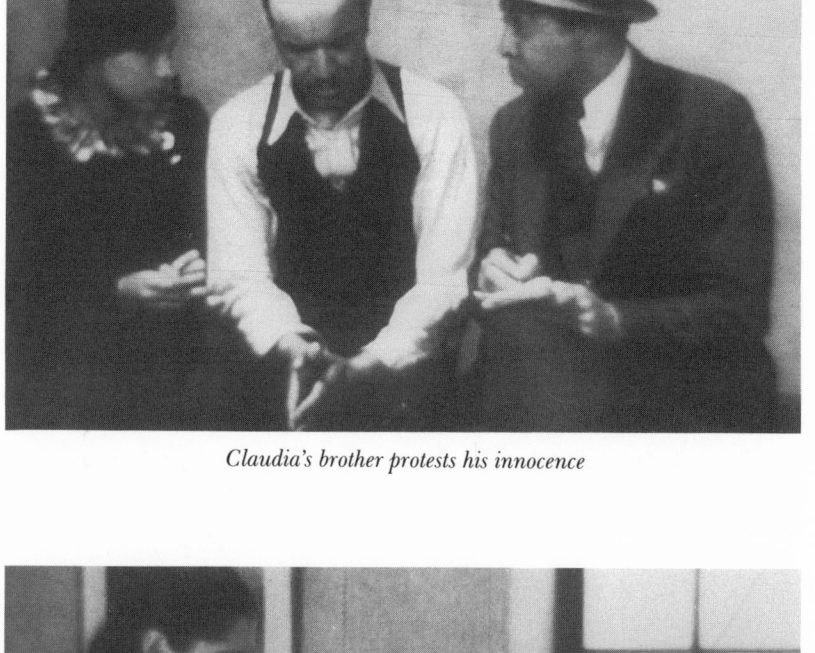

Claudia's brother protests his innocence

Mr. Brisbane sexually harasses his secretary.

Brisbane persuades Lem Hawkins to put the blame on the nightwatchman.

Claudia skillfully persuades Lem to talk.

Later, two detectives are examining the body and find two notes grasped in the dead woman's hand. One reads "He tell me lay down like night witch," and the other reads, "That tall Negro did this. He will try to lay it on the Night." They take the nightwatchman in on suspicion of murder.

At the station, a white police sergeant at the desk is booking the nightwatchman as a routine matter until he finds out that the victim was white, then he hurries off to find the Chief. While he is gone, the black detective sympathizes with the man's plea of innocence.

"That may be true," the detective says, "but the trouble will be getting these peckerwoods to believe it when they hear about it. The best thing, as I see it, is to slip you out of town for safekeeping before they find out about it."

TITLE CARD: "Behind every strange and mysterious murder, there is invariably always a story. To understand this, let us go back three years."

A man is selling books door-to-door, and tries his sales approach on a lady, telling her, "It's a fine new novel by a Negro author. Of course, everybody is ordering a copy, and why shouldn't they? A work like this by one of our group is something to order."

The good-natured lady orders a book. As an afterthought, she slyly directs him to a woman in the house across the street who is "always reading books."

Across the street in another apartment building, The Catbird is kissing her client goodbye, telling him that she wants to get back to her book. As the bookseller approaches, Claudia comes out of the apartment next door to The Catbird's establishment, and he assumes that Claudia is the woman he is meant to see. Intrigued by the novel—and by the bookseller, who introduces himself as "Henry Glory"—Claudia orders a book, to be delivered Saturday after five o'clock.

On Saturday, Henry delivers the ordered book to the lady. When he tells her that the woman across the street ordered a book, too, the lady shows surprise. When Henry wants to know why she is surprised at what the woman across the street does, the lady is evasive. Henry says he also met the young woman's mother.

"Mother?" she smirks. "That's sort of a nickname over there. All the girls call her 'mother.'"

Henry is perplexed, but the lady has a good laugh.

Across the street, Claudia seems glad to see Henry, and asks him in. Claudia's mother enters, is introduced to Henry, and wants to read the book first. As Henry has no more deliveries to make, Claudia asks him to sit down for awhile.

By comparing Henry's clean-shaven face to the picture of the mustached author in the book, Claudia discovers that Henry is actually the author. Asked why he remains anonymous, Henry replies:

"We belong to a not very appreciative group, when it comes to any achievement by each other, especially if they're privileged to meet that person, ordinarily. If many of the so-called "dicty" people, whom I must sell, thought I wrote the book, they wouldn't read it with an open mind." (NOTE: It should be obvious by now that the author Henry Glory has a lot in common with the author Oscar Micheaux, who would also sell his own books house-to-house and farm-to-farm.)

Henry tells her that the money he makes selling his books is financing his law education. Claudia suggests that he might want to practice in Washington, D.C., which "has no end of colored professional men."

"Is that so?" he queries. "I've always held just the opposite opinion. There's no industry in Washington to employ our group in the usual way, and—."

Claudia solves the mystery for Henry: "They marry themselves a school teacher, who, as you may have heard, are very well paid!"

Back at his book-buying friend's apartment, Henry confesses to her that he has fallen deeply in love with Claudia, and that he is going to call on her that night and tell her so. Then (probably because of the seeds of doubt the lady has sown in his mind about Claudia's 'profession'), he will go out of her life forever.

That night, Mrs. Vance is comforting her daughter, Claudia, who is totally and tearfully in love with Henry. They are overjoyed to see, through the window, that Henry is coming to see Claudia.

But before Henry can get to Claudia's door, he is waylaid by some of The Catbird's cronies who mistake him for a rich white man they have set up for a robbery. Henry is clubbed unconscious from behind. The robbers discover they've made a mistake when they find only seven dollars in his pocket.

"The wrong man—a Negro!" they exclaim, disgusted. "No wonder we didn't get nothing! A jig! The devil!"

Henry's unconscious form is disposed of, and he does not get to tell Claudia that he loves her after all.

TITLE CARD: "Now, we go three years forward in time."

Claudia enters a prestigious-looking law office and is surprised to find out that Henry Glory is now a very prosperous attorney. It seems that the nightwatchman in jail on suspicion of murdering the white secretary is her brother, and she is seeking legal aid for him. With some misgivings because she knows he hasn't been practicing long and she needs an experienced lawyer, Claudia hires Henry to defend her brother.

When Henry first questions him, the nightwatchman/brother is told that the murder probably happened about one or two o'clock in the afternoon before the body was discovered that midnight. At that time, he tells Henry, he had been summoned by Mr. Brisbane to the plant, then he was told to go home and come back five hours later.

(NOTE: The testimony of each character is told by flashbacks, in which we see the action as they describe it.)

At the preliminary hearings, Mr. Brisbane tells his version of the story: the secretary came in for her pay, then asked if certain chemical shipments had arrived. She went back to the storeroom to check. A few minutes later, Arthur the nightwatchman arrived and went to the storeroom to get some shoes he had left there. That was the last time Mr. Brisbane saw the girl alive.

"They'd indict anybody on that testimony," Henry tells Claudia, "but at the trial, it'll be different."

At the trial, Henry questions the slain secretary's mother, who tells the jury that the girl's boyfriend had tried earlier to get her pay from Mr. Brisbane, who had demanded that the girl herself come to get it. The boyfriend accompanied her to the plant, then came back without her at six o'clock that evening, asking where she was.

"I never saw her alive again," says the mother.

Back in Henry's office, Claudia tells him that she's very suspicious of Mr. Brisbane as the possible murderer, and that she has seen Brisbane exchanging glances with Lem Hawkins, the plant's janitor. She has her own plan to get more information.

After the trial is recessed the next day, Claudia starts following Lem. She hears him tell The Catbird that he will be at her big party the next night.

At the big party, Lem Hawkins arrives, dressed like a dandy. The Catbird apologizes that there is no table for him at the moment, but a young single girl nearby (Claudia) says:

"Sweet Papa can park himself here (at her table) if he's travelling alone. I'm all by myself—strange, sugar-cured, and single."

Lem doesn't need to be asked twice. While the band plays on, Claudia sees to it that Lem drinks straight "corn" while she stays sober, questioning him. As they are dancing, she compliments him for looking like a 'big shot.'

"I've got one of the easiest grafts of any jig in this town," he tells her proudly. Later, he adds that he knows a lot about this Mr. Brisbane and the murder trial, but that he's being paid plenty of money to keep his mouth shut. Just before he passes out, he says that Brisbane has promised him a whole lot of money and a ticket out of town when the trial is over.

The next day's newspapers tell of the arrest of Lem Hawkins as a material witness in the murder trial, and of his implication of his employer, Mr. Brisbane.

"Your intuition has put those two where they belong," Henry compliments Claudia, promising her "I'm going to grill the life out of Hawkins, and if I understand the heritage of our race, I'll make him talk!"

On the stand, Hawkins tells his version of the story.

Arriving at work, he is told by his boss that the secretary the boss has been hankering to make love to is finally within his grasp. He pays Lem to stand guard at the foot of the stairs while he has his way with the girl.

When the girl comes to get her back-salary from Brisbane, she also asks if some chemicals she ordered have arrived. He tells her she can look in the storeroom to see. Lem comes up the stairs and peeps through the keyhole to watch as Mr. Brisbane follows the girl into the storeroom. His peeping is interrupted, however, when a Mrs. Bates comes to see Brisbane, waits a few minutes, then leaves. By the time he gets back upstairs, Lem finds that it is all over. Brisbane tells him that the girl refused his advances, he hit her, and she fell with her head hitting something and is now unconscious. Brisbane tells Lem that he'll pay to have Lem's help in taking the girl somewhere else.

But when Lem goes into the storeroom to look at the girl, he finds that she is dead!

"They gonna lynch me sure when they finds out about this!" Lem moans to himself.

After he helps Brisbane take the body into the basement, Lem writes as Brisbane dictates the two notes which will be placed with the body. Then, Brisbane gives Lem $250 to go down and burn the girl's body in the furnace. When Lem refuses to do it, even after Brisbane's threats to have him lynched, Brisbane changes his mind and sends Lem across the street to a saloon "for some lunch." Instead of having lunch, Lem Hawkins drinks, and soon falls asleep, not to see Brisbane or the plant again until the morning after the body had been discovered. At that time, Lem tells the jury, Mr. Brisbane offered to pay him $50 per week to keep his mouth shut.

During a recess in the trial, Claudia brings in a young boy who lives near an old Mrs. Epps and her son. The son, who was the boyfriend of the murdered girl, often bragged to the young boy that he would someday break into the prison where Leopold and Loeb were being held and free them.

At old Mrs. Epps house, Henry threatens her with indictment if she doesn't tell him all she knows about her son's involvement with the murdered girl.

"I wanted to tell, but I was afraid," the old lady quavers. "I found him as a baby, a deserted child. He was marked—with the Brand of Cain!"

She says that, on the day of the murder, her son came home and told her all about it. In a flashback, we see what she heard. The Epps boy went with his girlfriend to get her pay from Brisbane. When she didn't come down after awhile, he went up the fire escape and—through the window—saw Brisbane trying to kiss her. By the time he made his way to the storeroom and found her lying on the floor but still alive, he thought she was bluffing, taunting him. So, he took a piece of rope and strangled her.

The next day, newspaper headlines tell how the Epps boy was shot while breaking into San Quentin Prison for some mysterious purpose—probably to help some prisoner friend escape.

In the book review section of the same newspaper, we also read of the publication of a new book by Henry Glory, entitled *A Fool's Errand*.

In her apartment, Claudia has gotten the book and is reading it. We see enough of it to know that it is autobiographical and that Henry is telling of how he fell in love with a "purple woman" who seemed like an angel, and was hit on the head for his reward.

Claudia sends him an urgent note to come see her that night. As he arrives, they see The Catbird out in the lobby talking loudly and drunkenly with one of her customers.

"That's the girl you've taken me for—for three years!" Claudia explains to Henry.

"I wonder if you can ever forgive me," Henry says, contritely. "I loved you then, I love you now, I will always love you."

By now, The Catbird is having a knock-down, drag-out fight with her client.

"My wedding present to you, dear, will be a new home," Henry promises her, "far, far from The Catbird's nest!"

Souls of Sin

CREDITS

Director: Powell Lindsay
Producer: William B. Alexander
Cinematographer: Louis Andres
Editor: Walter Kruder
Production Supervisor: Harriette A. Miller
Special Music: "The Things You Do to Me" by Savannah Churchill
and Henry Glover; "Lonesome Blues" and "No Good Blues" by
William Greaves
Year of Release: 1949
Running Time: 65½ minutes (5,878 ft.)

CAST

Regina: Savannah Churchill
Alabama: William Greaves
Dollar Bill: Jimmy Wright
Etta: Billie Allen
Roberts: Emery Richardson
Mrs. Sands: Louise Jackson
Bad Boy George: Powell Lindsay
Mac: Charley Mac Rae
Newspaper Editor: Bill Chase
Cool Breeze: Jesse Walter
Bartender & Dancing Patron: Harris & Scott

SYNOPSIS

Sharply-dressed William Burton (alias Dollar Bill) leaves the Harlem
street and enters a crowded basement apartment in a run-down tene-
ment. For furniture, there are three cots, a table with a radio and

Roommates in "the jungle"—as they call their room

Dollar Bill causes a disturbance in the bar.

Dollar Bill falls for Regina.

Bad Boy George gives Dollar Bill his assignment.

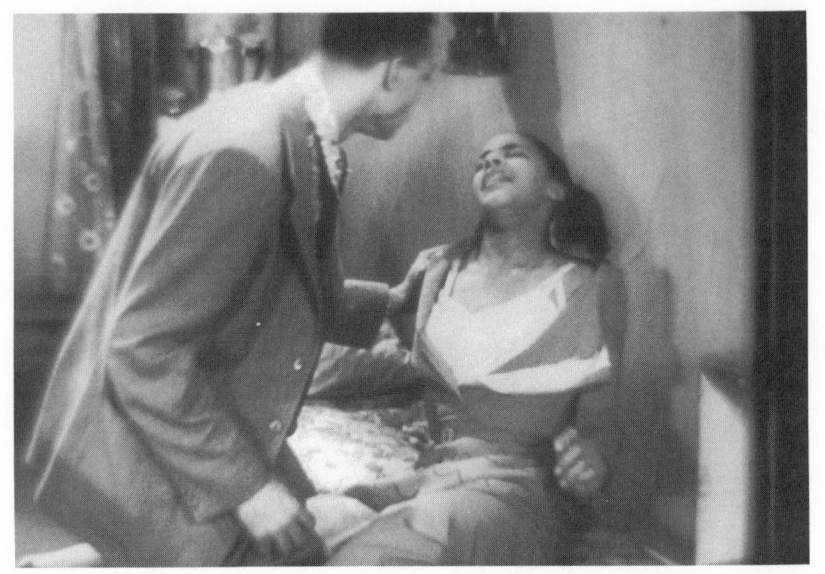

Dollar Bill repays Etta's love with violence.

Dollar Bill sells a worthless ring.

Fatally wounded, Dollar Bill staggers home to die.

Alabama goes on to fame.

another table with a typewriter. Bill turns on the radio to check the racing results and turns it off with a curse.

The landlady, Mrs. Sands, brings a new renter into the room and shows him the cot under the stairs. When he says he'll take it, she introduces him as "Mr. Isaiah Lee from Alabama," who quickly becomes Alabama. She introduces Dollar Bill as "a promoter," and the still-sleeping Roberts as "the no-writingest writer you'll ever meet."

While Alabama goes to wash his feet after his long journey, Bill hassles Mrs. Sands about adding yet another renter to their already-crowded room.

"He won't be here long," she retorts, "because he's a real winner—a working stiff, looking for a job. He's scared, maybe, but still in there with his dukes up."

"As far as I'm concerned," says Bill, "he's still a turkey, leading with his chin."

Alabama comes back in to find Dollar Bill checking the racing results again, and starts tapping on the typewriter. Bill pushes Alabama roughly away from the typewriter, telling him "that typewriter is (Roberts') life. Break that and you'll break his heart!"

To lighten the tension, Dollar Bill sees that Alabama has a guitar and asks him to play it. Flattered, Alabama plays and sings "like I do down in Muckroe County."

Roberts finally wakes up and gets to meet their new roommate. Alabama shyly offers his new friends the last of the chicken and biscuits his mother cooked for him to eat on the train, but they both refuse, claiming that good food might ruin their digestion. Alabama sings another song, which brings the landlady back down to tell them to cut out the racket.

Alabama goes out to eat at the local lunchroom, telling them he'll come back as soon as he has found a job.

"Come back anyway," Roberts tells him.

Although he has spoken almost sentimentally about Roberts to Alabama earlier, while Roberts was sleeping, when the wakeful old man starts telling Dollar Bill about a new idea for a story, it is too much for the angry young man.

"You're babbling like an imbecile," Bill rants, "talking about a story nobody's gonna buy while the whole world spits in your face! You dumb turkey! Peck away on that stinking typewriter until you rot! Go ahead! Sit here in this jungle like an animal, while the whole world steps on you! Well, nobody steps on Dollar Bill!"

Having worked himself into a frenzy, Bill storms out.

Dollar Bill comes into the neighborhood bar, where one of the customers makes the mistake of laughing at him because he's so poor. Bill throws a mug of beer in the man's face, then threatens to punch out the bartender when he refuses to serve Bill without seeing his money first. A fight begins over the debt, but it is stopped by a young woman (Etta) who offers to pay the check for Bill.

Later, in their room which they now call "The Jungle," Roberts is typing away. Dollar Bill comes in, still furious. Alabama tells them he has found a job at the lunchroom, washing dishes. When Etta, the young girl from the bar, comes in to see if Bill is okay, he thanks her as if he resented her help, and sends her away, crying.

The next morning, Mrs. Sands is talking with a neighbor lady about the best way to play a new variation of the numbers game when the postman brings yet another rejection slip for Roberts.

Downstairs, Etta has come in with a sackful of breakfast for everyone, but finds that only Roberts is there. In answer to his question about why she is so concerned with Dollar Bill, Etta explains that she was one of the little neighborhood kids who always idolized Bill, and to whom he used to give dollar bills. One time, when her mother was very sick, she used Bill's dollar to buy flowers for her mother.

"It was the last time I ever saw her smile," Etta says sadly.

Now, she is an orphan, but she lives with a lady-friend of the family and she has a good job in the Garment District.

Although Roberts thinks people do not come any better than Dollar Bill, he advises Etta that falling in love with him would be "like sticking your hand in a bag of loose needles."

In his drive to get to the top, Bill has chosen to work for Bad Boy George, who puts Bill to pushing stolen jewelry. In the bar, Bill meets a classy-looking lady named Regina, only to find out that she is Bad Boy George's girl. He sells a stolen ring to a man in the bar while Harris & Scott begin the film's "running gag" in which bartender Harris tries to keep patron Scott from dancing to the music of the juke box. Harris finally comes over the bar after Scott with a razor—a safety razor!

Bill returns to his room to find Etta there. Alabama excitedly tells them that Josh White likes his singing and has volunteered to give him free lessons. Bill is high on whiskey—and on Regina.

"I'm gonna move up to where people got class!" Dollar Bill declares. "Because I gotta breathe!"

"Well," drawls Roberts, "on your way back down, stop in The Jungle. Your friends will still be here."

At Bad Boy George's office, Bill receives $500 for his share in a recent heist, and gets his assignment for the robbery of a fur warehouse that night.

The next day, however, it turns out that Bill was being tailed by a police cruiser and was unable to shake them long enough to carry out his role in the robbery. Bad Boy George is angry with him, not only because he fouled up their robbery but also because he hears Bill has been getting too friendly with Regina.

A few days later, Dollar Bill is consorting very openly with Regina in the bar. She sings "their" song, "The Things You Do To Me," and winds it up with a big kiss for Bill. It is this moment which Bad Boy George chooses to enter. A fist-fight ensues between Dollar Bill and Bad Boy George in which Bill literally knocks George through the wall.

After the fight, Bill decides to pay a call on his old friends down in The Jungle, taking Regina with him. She has heard about Alabama and wants to hear him play. Despite the icy reception she gets from Etta, who is also there, Regina listens to Alabama's music with great interest. She invites Alabama back to the swanky night club where she sings so that he can play a number or two for her audience.

More time passes, and Bill pays another surprise visit to The Jungle. This time, he finds Etta there alone. When she tries to express how deeply she feels about him, Bill responds in a way she hadn't planned and tries to rape her. Roberts returns in time to put a stop to it.

At the club, Dollar Bill is confronted by the man to whom he sold the stolen ring, who wants his money back because the ring is worthless. Bill knocks the man down and returns to his drinking. But the man comes back in a few minutes with a gun and shoots Bill. As he falls, Bill shoots and kills the other man.

Badly wounded, Dollar Bill staggers through the streets of Harlem.

Meanwhile, in The Jungle, Alabama is excitedly telling Roberts and Etta about his good fortune. He has gotten a contract for $200 a week, for sixteen weeks, to be on a new television show. As they are drinking a bottle of wine the landlady has been saving for just such a moment, Dollar Bill drags himself in. With the last of his strength, he says, "I had to come back to The Jungle," and dies.

In a television studio, the announcer introduces "Alabama Ike and his guitar," and Alabama sings his "Lonesome Blues."

At a party afterwards in The Jungle, they are all celebrating Alabama's success when a telegram comes. Josh White, so the telegram says, has seen Alabama's show all the way down in Boston, and sends his congratulations. Mrs. Sands is as proud as if she were Alabama's mother.

During the celebration, the Editor of *The Harlem Herald* comes to see Roberts. He knows that Roberts was a friend of the late Dollar Bill, and wants the old man to write a series of articles about "Dollar Bill As I Knew Him." When Roberts proudly states that his writing probably would not be sensational enough for a newspaper, the Editor insists that that is just the kind of writing he wants, and that Roberts can write about any aspect of life in Harlem as he sees it.

Roberts and Alabama decide that, along with their newfound successes, they will need a secretary for Roberts and a manager for Alabama. They choose Etta, who happily accepts.

"But I only wish there were four of us to share all this success," she says sadly, thinking of Dollar Bill.

"That's life," philosophizes Roberts, "for every ending, there's a beginning."

By-Line Newsreels

Producers: William Alexander and Biddy Woods
Director: William Alexander
Narrator/Interviewer: William Alexander
Year of Release: 1953–56
Running Time:
Number 1: 7½ minutes (648 ft.)
Number 2: 6 minutes (540 ft.)
Number 3: 7½ minutes (675 ft.)
Number 4: 7 minutes (612 ft.)

SYNOPSES: BY-LINE NEWSREEL 1

WASHINGTON, D.C.: Shots of Colville Richardson, Chairman of the Federal Parole Board and the first Negro ever appointed to the Board, and of Howard Jenkins and Roberta Church, who were both appointed by President Eisenhower to important Labor Department positions.

BALTIMORE, MARYLAND: Thirty-six Marine Reservists, both black and white, embark by train for the Marine Base at Paris Island for six months' training. General James Devereaux of Wake Island fame is there to see them off, as are their families and sweethearts. When this training is completed, they will spend the rest of their reserve enlistments as members of the First Engineer Battalion from Baltimore.

SPORTS: At Baltimore's Memorial Stadium, the favored Chicago Bears meet the Baltimore Colts. On opposing sides are Negro stars Lenny Moore for Baltimore (an ex of Penn State) and Bobby Watkins for Chicago (an ex of Ohio State). Fans numbering 45,000 see the Colts upset the Bears, 28-21.

"The Continentals" at a Maryland resort

COMMUNITY AFFAIRS: The Washington, D.C., chapter of "The Continentals" host representatives from all other Eastern seacoast chapters for a last outing of the season at a Colton, Maryland resort. The weekend is highlighted by a party at the smart country home of the Charles Jacksons.

NEW YORK CITY: Chorus girls Pat, Mary, and Alice show off their new costumes and "Ike" buttons. Fashion models Dorothea Toll, Mary Cunningham, and Frances Wallace walk down Fifth Avenue sporting their "Let's Back Ike" buttons. A tiny elephant, "an old Ike supporter," wears an "I Like Ike" banner.

NATIONAL AFFAIRS: At the offices of the U.S. Mission to the United Nations in New York City, we visit with Mrs. Carmel Carrington Marr, Advisor on Political and Legal Affairs for the mission. She explains her work as liaison with the other 75 delegations. There are few questions in the U.N. which come up without legal aspects to them, and as representative of the host nation, she helps the delegations deal with these matters.

Altus Air Force Base: "The Story of a Hand"

BY-LINE NEWSREEL 2

NATIONAL AFFAIRS: In Baltimore, folks of all races who are proud of their heritage join in the "I'm an American Day" parade.

ALTUS AIR FORCE BASE: In the armed forces, fully integrated by President Eisenhower, there are many heart-warming stories. This is "The Story of A Hand." T/Sgt. Herman Roberts (black) notices jet aircraft mechanic James Travis (white) at work on a jet engine. When he sees the difficulty Travis has manipulating the tools with the artificial claw apparatus he has for a right hand, Sgt. Roberts goes into the base machine shop and fashions a better hand, with sockets and braces to hold Travis' tools. They replace the old claw with the new prosthetic hand, and there is no more dropping of tools.

WASHINGTON, D.C.: Coming out of their government office buildings, we see top black appointees Julia Cooper (first woman member of the Criminal Division of the Justice Department); Philip Sadler (public housing and race relations advisor); Alexander Lanaville (Special

Assistant in the Veterans' Administration); Samuel Pierce (lawyer in the Anti-Trust Division of the Justice Department and Assistant to the Undersecretary of Labor). We also see three men who have been assigned to important Post Office positions: Joel Birch, Vernon Green, and Joseph Clark.

WASHINGTON, D.C.: William Alexander interviews a "Mr. Hayes" (no first name given), who is Chairman of the Commission of Public Utilities. Mr. Hayes explains his job directing the office, which regulates gas, electricity, telephone, taxicab, and other transit services in the District of Columbia in an effort to maintain a system of fairness between the community and the various utilities.

ENTERTAINMENT: Backstage at the famous Havana Club in New York City's Greenwich Village, which is noted for its beautiful and talented line of chorus girls, we see the ladies preparing to go onstage. Then, we see a bit of the show.

BY-LINE NEWSREEL 3

NATIONAL AFFAIRS: In Washington, D.C., By-Line News visits with E. Frederick Morrow, one of President Eisenhower's top aides. Mr. Morrow states: "My job is one of the most dramatic symbols of the Eisenhower philosophy of democracy, where a man should have the right to rise in the world as far as his ambition, character and preparation can carry him. Neither President Eisenhower nor I had any desire for me to come to Washington to do the thing customarily expected of Negro office-holders—that of being an advisor on racial matters. When a president believes in one kind of first-class citizenship for all citizens, he does not need advice on how to mete out any special kinds of treatment or attention to the Negro segment of the population. Consequently, my job is of the same consequence and responsibility of any of his administrative assistants. By the same token, the President has granted me the same emoluments and privileges of office that he has granted to all other assistants."

Next, By-Line visits in the office of Lois Lippman, first Negro member of the White House staff. In doing regular secretarial duties since

William Alexander interviews E. Frederick Morrow.

William Alexander interviews Lois Lippman.

1953, at the beginning of the Eisenhower administration, she tells of working with Sherman Adams, Nelson Rockefeller, Fred Seaton, and Charles Willis. She is presently secretary to Thomas Pike. She hails from Boston originally, but worked for the original Eisenhower campaign in New York City.

Also in Washington, By-Line visits with J. Earnest Wilkins, Assistant Secretary of Labor, who tells of his many responsibilities as the U.S. Representative to the International Labor Organization, Chairman of the Interdepartmental Committee on International Labor Policy, and many other organizational duties within the Department of Labor.

SPORTS: Top-notch U.S. Airmen are on hand at the Los Angeles Memorial Coliseum for qualification in the U.S. Track and Olympic field trials. George Mathes falls short of the Reverend Bob Richards' pole vaulting accomplishment, but gets a second berth. Other qualifiers among the Air Force athletes are Thane Baker, Tom Lee, Lon Spurrier, and Jerry Smart.

COMMUNITY AFFAIRS: (a repeat of "The Continentals" segment of Newsreel #1)

BY-LINE NEWSREEL 4

NATIONAL AFFAIRS: (a repeat of the Baltimore "I'm An American Day" parade)

SAN FRANCISCO: In the Cow Palace, the Republican National Convention is in high gear. Former New York governor, Thomas Dewey, speaks to a rousing ovation. By-Line interviews top Negroes who play key parts in the convention. Dr. Helen Edmonds, as a specialist in history, evaluates the Eisenhower/Nixon team as above any in our century, and it is her fervent prayer that they will go on to greater heights. Hobson Reynolds of Philadelphia remembers that three and one-half years ago, he was the one who seconded Eisenhower's nomination, and predicted he would become the best president since Lincoln. "He has lived up to that prediction by representing 500,000 Negroes in America through the Civil Liberties Department, and we're going all-out for his re-election." Patricia Ann Spaulding is one of sixteen girl usherettes for the convention's V.I.P.'s, and she wants a continuation of the Eisenhower/Nixon leadership so that "peace, prosperity and progress" can continue. Olympic star Mal Whitfield testifies that he is happy to be in the Eisenhower administration, and that the Civil Rights program will eventually do what it is designed to do, making the U.S. a country which other nations will look up to. Finally, Mrs. Feldon Sparks of Alaska is interviewed, and she hopes that President Eisenhower is elected, "because he kept my boys out of war and I know he will continue for peace."

SPORTS: At the Morgan State College stadium, the Morgan Bears collide with the North Carolina State team in the opening CIAA game of the season. It is a 6-6 tie.

At Ebbets Field in Brooklyn, the World Series begins as President Eisenhower throws out the first ball to Dodger catcher Roy Campanella.

Other Short Films in the Collection

Broken Earth

CREDITS

Director: Roman Freulich
Producer: Continental Pictures, Inc.
Screenwriter: Roman Freulich
Associate Producer: Andrew V. White
Assistant Director: Henry Spitz
Cinematographers: Jerome Ash, King Grey
Sound: Hans Wieren
Editor: George McGrath
Musical Director: Freida Shaw
Year of Release: 1939
Running Time: 11 minutes (998 ft.)

CAST

Joshua: Clarence Muse
Little Joshua: (unidentified)
Field Hands: (unidentified)

SYNOPSIS

A man named Joshua is plowing his field in the broiling sun. As he guides the mule, he passes a spot where several other men are resting in the shade of a big tree, singing "All God's Chillun Got Shoes." They shout greetings to him, but he goes on plowing.

When he does take a break, he goes to his little one-room shack nearby and tends to his sick child, Little Joshua, assuring him that he is going to be all right soon. Joshua rinses and changes a cool cloth for the child's fevered brow, but has no other medicine to give him.

Joshua walks up into the field behind the house where his wife is buried. He talks to her grave, assuring her that Little Joshua is going to get well—"he's all we've got."

Back at the house, Little Joshua rouses long enough to call for

"Pappy!" but then falls back, unconscious. Their little dog, Coffee, senses that something is wrong with the child, and goes to find Joshua. Coffee finds Joshua on the other side of the hill, plowing, and barks and tugs at his pants-leg until Joshua realizes something is wrong and follows the little dog to the shack.

Joshua finds Little Joshua unconscious, and changes the cool cloth on his brow again, pleading for him to wake up. Then, he prays for mercy (as the Freida Shaw Choir sings "Swing Low, Sweet Chariot" on the soundtrack).

"Oh Lord, I'm a poor pilgrim of sorrow," Joshua prays, "tossed in this wide, wide world, with no hope for the morrow. My poor wife is gone to that pure glory, and here I am, still walking in fear. My brothers and sisters, they won't own me, because I'm trying, Lord, trying. Trying to get in!"

A strong ray of sunlight breaks through the clouds over the little cabin. Slowly, Little Joshua opens his eyes, and Joshua, overcome with joy, sings "I've Heard of a City Called Heaven."

Joshua plows his field.

Joshua visits his wife's grave.

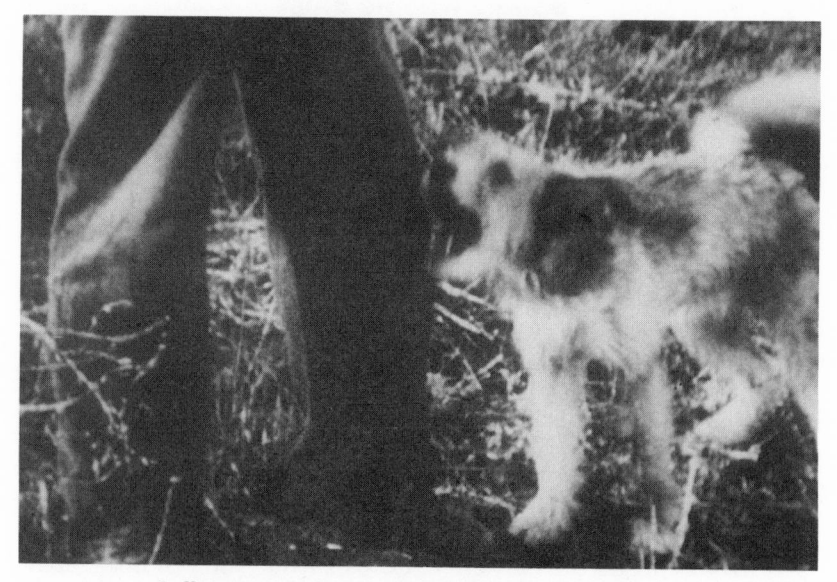

Coffee tugs at Joshua's pants-leg to get him to come home.

Joshua prays over Little Joshua.

Boogie Woogie Blues

CREDITS
Director: Uncredited
Producer: All-American News, Inc.
Year of Release: 1948
Running Time: 10 minutes (900 ft.)

CAST
Hadda Brooks, vocalist/pianist

SYNOPSIS
Ms. Brooks, accompanying herself on the piano, sings several songs: "Don't Take Your Love From Me," "Don't You Think I Ought To Know?," and "I'm Tired Of Everything But You." Although the set is only one living-room location, the cool beauty and low, sultry voice of Miss Brooks makes the film a delight. Of further interest is the manner in which the director obviously tries to "stretch" the three numbers into filling one "reel" of film: several times he has her reprise a final chorus of a number that she has obviously ended, even after we hear the director yelling "cut!" off-screen.

Hadda Brooks at the piano.

Bare-footed tap dancer

Hauling bananas to the docks

Cora Harris

The Red Lilly Chorus

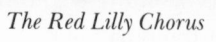

Stringbeans Jackson

Daughters of the Isle of Jamaica

CREDITS
Producer: Lenwall Productions
Year of Release: 1937
Running Time: 8½ minutes (739 ft.)

CAST
(Uncredited)

SYNOPSIS

The film opens in a Kingston nightclub, where the emcee introduces a very special tap dancer—it is a young Jamaican boy who tap dances barefooted by holding bottle caps between his toes!

The film then goes outdoors for a trip through Kingston and the surrounding territory: we see black workers crushing rocks to make a new roadway, climbing coconut trees to bring down the fruit, cutting bananas and hauling them to the docks on their heads (where a supervisor with a machete hair-raisingly slashes at their loads, front and back, to remove excess stalk), riding burros to market, and finally, we see the famous waterfalls.

Harlem Hot-Shots

CREDITS
Director: Uncredited
Producer: Alfred N. Sack
Year of Release: 1940
Running Time: 8 minutes (727 ft.)

CAST

Leon Gross and His Orchestra
Cora Harris
The Red Lilly Chorus
Stringbeans Jackson

SYNOPSIS

To begin this nightclub-type performance film, Leon Gross and his Orchestra perform "Swingeroo Stomp" and then accompany Cora

Harris as she sings "Heaven Help This Heart Of Mine." The Red Lilly Chorus does a tap number entitled "Dance of the Bellhops," and the finale is a spirited 'specialty dance' by Stringbeans Jackson.

Junior Jeeps

CREDITS

Executive Producer: George Weiss
Narrator: Edward Mason
Continuity: Sam Elljay
Cinematographer: Hal Malvern
Sound: Melvin D'Anton
Year of Release: 1947
Running Time: 10 minutes (910 ft.)

CAST

Uncredited

SYNOPSIS

A young man reads in a newspaper of an up-coming auto race at the local track—Bonelli Stadium. He shows the notice to a younger friend, and they begin to dream of being racedrivers themselves. Walking through the neighborhood, they spy an old race car at a garage. Through much eloquent arguing and bargaining, they manage to talk the owner out of the machine. He even helps them to fix it up. They enter the race, with the younger boy driving, and their fantasy is fulfilled as he wins!

The boys find an old race car.

They pretend they are in a race.

The crowd goes wild as they win.

Vanities

CREDITS

Director: William Alexander
Producer: William Alexander
Year of Release: 1946
Running Time: 10 minutes (900 ft.)

CAST

Charles Keith
Joesfred Portee
Audrey Armstrong

SYNOPSIS

This is another nightclub performance film, with young Charles Keith
as Master of Ceremonies. Before he introduces the other acts, he confesses that he is an out-of-work actor whose idol is Bette Davis. He does
a masterful impersonation of her role in *The Letter* in which he first
sounds remarkably like the actress, then even begins to look like her.

The next act is Joesfred Portee, who sings "I Love My Daddy, But
I've Got to Have My Fun." Then, Keith introduces "Little Audrey"

Armstrong, who demonstrates her remarkable muscle control and persistence in a gyrating dance. For a finale, Ms. Portee comes back and sings, "On the Solid Side."

Charles Keith impersonates Bette Davis.

Joesfred Portee sings.

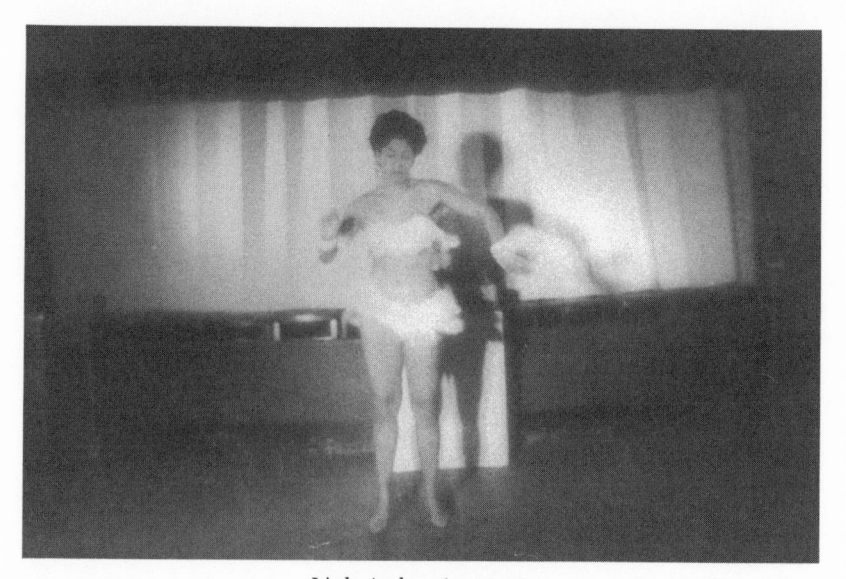

Little Audrey Armstrong

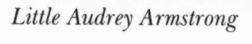

Comments from Some of Today's Black Filmmakers

The following comments are derived largely from a series of seminars held at the Meadows School of the Arts, Southern Methodist University, in February of 1985, upon the occasion of the first screenings of restored prints from the "Tyler, Texas, Black Film Collection." Leaders of the seminars included Dr. Barbara Bryant, a filmmaker and film distributor, vice-president of Phoenix Films of New York City; Mr. Ossie Davis, author, actor and film and television producer-director; Mr. William Greaves, a film and video producer-director with his own company in New York City, who formerly acted in many of the black-audience films of the 1940s including *Souls of Sin* and *Miracle in Harlem*; Mr. Harrel Gordon Tillman, attorney and former judge in Houston, who also acted in many of the black-audience films of the 1940s; Mr. Herman Abrams, a retired film distributor who formerly headed the Dallas office of Ted Toddy Productions; and Professor Gregory Adams, a Visiting Assistant Professor in Communications at Prairie View A & M University in Prairie View, Texas.

How the Films Were Produced, Distributed, Exhibited— and What Became of the System

Making the Black-Audience Films in the Forties

WILLIAM GREAVES: You have to recognize that America in the 1940s was not unlike what I tend to think South Africa is today. It was a very racist society, so that the black performing artists had feelings of anxiety and tension brought on by this general climate. Not that

William Greaves and Harold Tillman at the Black Film seminar

everyone who was white in these situations was racist, but one was always aware of this hostile racial climate. On the set of a picture like *Souls of Sin,* however, there were black people behind the camera as well as in front of the camera, and there was a feeling of relaxation. Having said that, though, I think I could say that the white technical and production people were generally positive about working with black talent.

As far as my memory serves me, I never saw a black technician behind the cameras during that time. You have to remember that the country was a different country than it is today. Always, on the nontechnical side of motion picture production, there were people like Bill Alexander, Oscar Micheaux, Noble Johnson. You had various people who were in the writing of motion pictures, like Spencer Williams— who also directed. But even there, it was largely a white situation.

The problem of black people becoming included in filmmaking crews as technicians was complicated by the fact that there simply was not that level of training and expertise within the black community. The business of making a film, of operating the cameras and being sensitive to all the technology of film production, requires a degree of training. That training was absolutely denied to black talent through the unions, although there was some opportunity through the rare educational institutions which were teaching film technology then. As a matter of fact, I started studying film production about that same time, in 1950, at City College in New York. There were only two schools in the United States which were involved then in the actual training of technicians: the University of Southern California and City College of New York. If you didn't go to those schools you just had no way of learning, no matter what your ethnic background was, except through the union system. But the unions were implacably hostile to the inclusion of black technical people on the crews. So there was just no way. In order to complete my training beyond my years at college, I had to leave America in 1952. I stayed out of the country for eleven years, working in film production in Canada.

Even if there had been no restrictions from the unions, trying to use black people in those jobs behind the camera would have been like trying to launch a spaceship in a country which has no frame of reference for that type of expertise. We were kept absolutely out of those areas.

BARBARA BRYANT: The black independent films did open a lot of doors for the black artists. Within the Hollywood system, it was very difficult for young blacks to participate even as extras and—in a repertory sense—begin to learn their craft, either as actors or directors or writers. Not every young black artist was going to become a Lena Horne or an Ossie Davis or a Ruby Dee, and get a chance to walk through the Hollywood door, but in the independent black films, more young people had a chance to make an entrance.

OSSIE DAVIS: The actors in even the black independent films knew that they were being exploited, both by the black producers and by the white ones. The actors had to learn how to live by their wits and to resist such exploitation on a personal basis. I guess they just negotiated the price up to where they knew it was as much as they could get, and then they stuck to that. The actors were their own agents—in other words, they negotiated the highest price they could get and then they were prepared if the producer or the manager was going to skip town without paying them. That was a part of what acting was like in that day, and it was more a part of it for black performers if they wanted to be included in motion pictures, even at that particular level.

Dr. Barbara Bryant

I think that the basic problem that communicators face, both then and now, in a minority community, is how to make sure that—whatever the audience sees you do—to make sure they laugh with you and not at you. It's a very subtle and delicate line and sometimes you fall over onto the wrong side. But that is always a constraint, particularly among black actors and producers. How much can we reveal of the inner aspects of our lives without giving those who would oppress us added ammunition to further oppress us? Sometimes, we would present ourselves as being holier than holy, more middle-class than middle-class, more righteous than anybody else, trying to counteract that negative stereotype. From what I see of these films, the problem was resolved positively. There is still an energy, still an attractiveness to them that makes you want to watch, and to empathize with the people represented by those actors.

WILLIAM GREAVES: The investors in the independent black films were largely white. Bill Alexander had access to black investment capital, and I believe that Oscar Micheaux had access to black capital; but largely it was people like the Goldberg brothers, whose money was white money. The Jewish community at that particular time was not the way we understand the Jewish community today, when it is very fully-integrated into the whole fabric of the economic and political structures of this country. At that time, there was a high incidence of anti-Semitism in America, and there was the exclusion of Jewish businessmen and Jewish political figures throughout the whole length and breadth of this country. So, the Jewish community identified much more fully with the struggles of the black community then, when it was really fighting for its life in this country. The Jewish community, having had the experience of the Nazi regime in Germany, had a basis for empathy with the black community. It also had, interestingly, an acceptance by the black community from a business perspective, so that a lot of Jewish business activity began within the black community. There was an empathy, born out of socio-historical-political realities, that caused the two communities to bind together, that permitted Jewish business people to function in the black community when they couldn't have functioned like that within the mainstream white communities.

BARBARA BRYANT: Oscar Micheaux was one of the producers who did get the major part of his financing from the black community. One of the things he began to do, once he was initially financed, was to put the picture into distribution and go back home, write his next film, and then the money he earned from the film then in distribution would be used to finance his next film. That was how he kept his finances, his revenue, generated—by using profits from that which he had done before. And, from time to time when he would need to have more money invested from the community, he would simply go from state to state, particularly in the South. Atlanta provided him with a tremendous amount of money. Surprisingly, so did parts of Alabama and the northern part of Texas.

Distribution of the Films

HERMAN ABRAMS: The black-audience films had, in comparison to the majority of other films, a limited market. In Dallas, for instance, there were only three companies which were into distribution of these films, and the Ted Toddy organization was the largest of them. Although he was based primarily in New York City, his production unit for these films, in Atlanta, was known as the Dixie National Company. Much of the money that he earned in distributing his other pictures, such as his westerns and other specialty pictures, he invested in making the black films, because he simply loved to make black films. He had a certain feeling in his heart for black people. At that time, he actually had most of the black films that were in release. In 1948, he projected a series of eight independently-made films. He had stars with his company like Pigmeat Markam and Mantan Moreland. They were great comedy people and he loved that type of entertainment. He loved seeing it, he loved producing it, and he loved the idea that there were audiences waiting to get that kind of film. The owners of black theaters tried their best to get the kind of films that the people were interested in. There were black theater owners and also white theater owners. There was nothing to distinguish the way we did business with either of them, because it was the audiences that counted. You had a large population of black people who were hungry for any kind of film that would give them a realistic experience of their own culture.

Why Did the Black-Audience Films Die Out?

BARBARA BRYANT: Integration. I can remember my great-grandmother saying, when the move towards integration began, that she didn't know whether this was going to be a really good thing or not. She was a profoundly religious, deeply-rooted, well-disciplined Methodist. Within the Methodist Episcopal Church at that time, blacks had their own bishops, their own leaders, and she could see them losing those positions because of integration. There would at least be a power struggle and blacks were not only a minority within the nation, but also within the Methodist Church. Well, the same thing occurred with integration and the film. There were more blacks being included in white films, and there was a promise and a hope that this was going to become a bigger reality as integration progressed. Some of the people who had been supplying money for the black films began to die or became less energetic, and there was no one there to pick up the commitment they had previously had. So, optimism about integration and the hope of real change—which never came about—was one of the reasons the whole attitude toward black independent filmmaking dried up, not to re-emerge strongly until Melvin Van Peebles.

WILLIAM GREAVES: There was the fact of integration that was taking place, and the need of the black community to become a part of America in the fuller sense of the term. And there was the clear need and persistence of some black actors like Jimmy Edwards, Dotts Johnson, or Canada Lee in these movies which were largely white that signaled to the black community a willingness and an interest, on the part of the larger American family, to include black people in their reality. There was a rush out of the ghettos to the downtown theaters to see Sidney Poitier or Ossie Davis or various other black stars who had begun to appear in these films.

A further complicating factor in the production of black independent films at that time was the rising costs. You could no longer make a feature for from eight to twenty thousand dollars. The actual theaters themselves in the black neighborhoods were being torn down because of escalating real estate values, and other kinds of structures were going up. The union costs were going up. Costs all across the board were going up, so that while you might be able to get a certain amount of financing—say fifteen to thirty thousand dollars—to do a black film in 1947, by 1953 that money had to be somewhere in the vicinity of eighty to a hundred thousand dollars. Today, there's no way I can even think of a budget that's under two million dollars.

OSSIE DAVIS: Integration did dislocate many of the structures we had in our communities by which we expressed ourselves economically, culturally, religiously, and otherwise, and that is a factor of some account. But I think that another factor we often forget is that America is essentially market-oriented. As the Hollywood system grew larger, it grew greedier for markets—among blacks and everyone else. There was the urge to push aside the independent. Perhaps an example of this more easily understood comes from what happened in the days when there used to be a large number of "Mom and Pop" grocery stores in all the communities. But then the giant chains came into the same communities, cut the prices so that the smaller stores could not compete, and then snuffed them out. Now, you see in all the communities—not the Mom and Pop stores which catered to the individual needs of the community, which served as the training-ground for young people to learn business, which provided credit on the basis of personal relationship and trust—but the chain stores, which are headquartered God-knows-where and in which you're not known by a person but by a computer. These chain stores came into the communities like television came between us filmmakers and our audiences, and we have to take this into account to understand why such a vital and significant contribution to the culture of the country—the independent black film—was ultimately snuffed out.

The black musician today has to compete with the disco and the record stores, owned not by him but by someone else. The fact is still in operation, and it operates first on black people. Ten or twenty years later, it also gets white people. That's one of the beauties of the black experience: it shows the whites what's coming—although the whites don't thoroughly understand that yet.

What Black Independent Films Meant
to the Black Community

WILLIAM GREAVES: In order to appreciate what the black independent films meant to audiences back in the thirties and the forties, you have to go back to the middle of the last century, when the struggle for freedom was taking place on the part of the Afro-American. There was the abolitionist movement and the anti-abolitionist movement, and there was a tremendous vilification campaign that was launched by the anti-abolitionists to discredit the black people of this country, to vilify them. In other words, to make it philosophically correct to oppress black people. The media were brought into collusion with the anti-abolitionists and a great deal of literature and a lot of general information about black people which went out to the American public was of a very derogatory nature. You got an excessive reliance upon the buffoon, the black comic—all of the various images which are stereotypical and which, in one way or another, caused people to feel superior to black people and, at the same time, quite insensitive to any oppression to which the black people were being subjected.

That legacy of media vilification has, of course, generally receded. But there are still traces of it, even today. Just recently, the Civil Rights Commission did a study on black images on television—network television—and one of the curious features of that report was that they found American television to have an inordinately large incidence of black males in comedy situations. Whenever you saw a black male on television, it would be within the context of comedy. The study found that the black male is not taken that seriously by the media, even today. There's a legacy of that whole period. Similarly, there are other findings in this report, called "Window Dressing on the Media," that reveal these trends so that, in terms of marketing of black people, if there is a predisposition on the part of large segments of the population to popularize that type of film or television, then whoever has the money and whoever can invest in the movies will invest in these kinds of movies, you see, because they play right along with that particular motif in American life.

OSSIE DAVIS: If I could speak to the issue of images as they appeared to a little black boy who lived in Waycross, Georgia: what did movies really do—what did they mean in our lives?

Bear in mind that movies are a part of the mythology of the times—not the reality of the times. These two worlds can be quite different and can serve quite different purposes. When we went to see movies as individuals or as groups, we couldn't wait until we got to the schoolgrounds to share with each other what the movies were about. If the movie was Tom Mix chasing the Indians, we chased the Indians, too. (When we saw black folks in the Westerns at that particular time, usually the parts were so derogatory that we identified with the Indians rather than with the blacks!) When we heard Bing Crosby singing "Sweet Lelani," we would sing that, too. On the other hand, when we heard Nat "King" Cole sing "Sweet Lorraine," we would sing that, too.

When we had a chance to see black films and we got together to talk with each other about the films, we were able to have a place in the dominant mythology of the times. In the black cowboy story, we saw no black folks serving or running or whatever—we saw black people in chaps and spurs and with guns on, who knew how to get on a horse and how to ride off and catch the villain and knock the living day-lights out of him. This was an important corrective for us. We were not exposed only to the absence of positive black images in the regular Hollywood fare—the black films were an antidote for that. As I re-member, we lived out all of the films—*Frankenstein* and *King Kong*. What we did was to internalize the mythology of the times and make it into a form that didn't damage our self-concept. Without those black films as I remember them, and without the black radio where we could hear Duke Ellington, or without those short films where we could see Cab Calloway, we would have been seriously damaged in terms of what we got from the Westerns and the motion pictures where Bing Crosby was singing to the whites and somebody black was carrying a bale of cotton on his head in the background.

So, in terms of what those images meant to us, they were our way of stating in our own language that we, too, were somebody—that we had an important place in the public mythology by which definitions about important events were being made. They were invaluable to us.

HARREL TILLMAN: During that time, I remember a person whom I don't think anybody has mentioned yet—Ralph Cooper—who was really the Clark Gable of the black motion picture. Ralph Cooper was a handsome, strapping man. He did not look at all like the Hollywood image of a leading man, but he was what the black image was. Just as Edna Mae Harris did not look like Lana Turner. Consequently, we had a different idea, when we would go to see a film with Ralph Cooper or Edna Mae Harris in it. We would see the type of person that we saw among our own girlfriends and like we saw in ourselves. Ralph Cooper was a little stockier than Jimmy Stewart, and a little more flamboyant. He was the reverse-image of what the white leading men were. He'd play everything—he was the black James Cagney at one time—as he was in *Bullets or Ballots*.

Anyway, a long time ago, seeing those black actors and actresses on the screen gave us an idea that we could be like that. Ralph Cooper wore his hair plastered to his head, so I went and got a bottle of Vase-line and plastered my hair down like Ralph Cooper did. My father wanted to kill me when he came home from church (my father was a minister) and saw me with my hair plastered down like that. He said,

"What is wrong with you?" and made me go immediately and wash that Vaseline out of my hair.

As I say, we could empathize—we could reflect that person. We even reflected Herbert Jeffries, who was an outstanding singer but a bad actor. Nobody could touch him singing "Flamingo." He was also a tall, strapping man. We could just see ourselves being like him in *Harlem on the Prairie*. We, too, could ride the range with Mantan Moreland as our sidekick—not Gabby Hayes, but Mantan Moreland. This gave us the opportunity to bask in reflected glory.

I had a bit of a different perspective, however, because I was very fortunate to have been acquainted with a man who was a minister in my father's church—a man who was an ordained preacher in the church. I knew him, because one of the bishops in this African Methodist Episcopal Zion Church used to carry this man around with him. The man was Paul Robeson. I had an opportunity to elevate my consciousness because of the fact of knowing Paul Robeson, who was also in black films, and who transcended all the barriers. Because Paul Robeson was Mister Everything—he was the ideal, he was the American Dream. Here's a man who was the epitome of all America wants all its males to be, and he was vilified and castigated. By talking with him, he gave me another perspective on what things were about. He told me not to get carried away by this fantasy and this mystique that Ossie was talking about. I'm sure all of us wanted to be like those motion picture heroes, both white and black; but Paul brought me back to reality because he told me that, with all the talent that he had, he was suffering.

BARBARA BRYANT: I grew up in a very censurious family as far as what we saw in the form of movies, and—when television became a reality—as far as what we were allowed to see on television. My mother thought she was always choosing very wisely, but she didn't have a very bright older daughter. She was eavesdropping on us one day when I was with a group of children and saying, "I'm going to grow up to be June Allyson!"

I heard a "Barbara! Come into this house!" and I said, "Oh, God! What have I done now?"

It took her a long time before she could say anything to me, but finally she said, "I have tried to provide you with alternatives. I have tried to provide you with a right direction. There is no way you're going to grow up to be June Allyson! You're already taller than she is and you're only ten years old! And look in the mirror—you are not a blonde! Just imagine yourself as a blonde, and have nightmares!"

But I had also been seeing all the black films. My family worked in Hollywood, and I had aunts and uncles who both acted in films and were musicians for them, so I had an awareness. But what was happening to me at that time was the overwhelmingness of that other imagery—the white imagery. My mother began to censor what I experienced even more. When *Song of the South* came out, I remember that I was totally forbidden to see it. She felt that the imagery was not going to be something I needed to see, because I was a little weird and very impressionable. I reflect now on how the balance really began to happen—with my mother and my aunts and my uncles pounding in on me—and being exposed to people like Herb Jeffries and Dinah Washington and Ella Fitzgerald, to people who did play clowns, like Mantan Moreland and Eddie Anderson. But I knew them in a different context. I had seen the black films, and in the black films, when a comic was being a comic, it was against a perspective which was balanced by the fact that he was being comical with other black people who were being sane, in control, and acting the roles of substantial citizens. I never once lost respect for their comic ability, because I had seen it in these films. It was the same thing with Amos n' Andy—I could never understand what the furor was about, because I had always from childhood seen the black comedians in black settings. They may have been behaving in a buffoonish manner, but everyone else around them was also black, but sophisticated and normal.

So, all of those images affected how I thought about myself, and how I was going to present that information to my children. I did not censor and, fortunately, there is now enough information to provide them with some alternatives. But how I saw myself growing up as June Allyson, even with experience and exposure to different alternatives, it was just amazing!

WILLIAM GREAVES: I think that, in that period, Joe Louis and people like Marian Anderson, Paul Robeson and—to a lesser extent—Canada Lee were people who were deeply revered within the black community. I don't think there was really a basis of comparison between them and most of the white performers as hero images, for the simple reason that we did a lot of our living through these heroes. I mean, we *really* identified with them—Marian Anderson, George Washington Carver. What we're talking about is, on the one hand from the standpoint of spectators or fans, we'd go to the movies to see Clark Gable or Jean Harlow—but when it came to really personal heroes, people that you can put up on the wall like icons, it was Marian Anderson or Paul Robeson. It was people like that that one really strongly identified with.

It's interesting, the problems of perception that go on in America from various groups. While the black community did enjoy seeing Cab Calloway, for instance, there was no feeling for Cab Calloway of the kind that one associates with a Paul Robeson or a Marian Anderson, or any of those other, major artists. For the black community, Cab Calloway was skating very close to the edge of certain types of stereotypical images that the black community was very anxious about avoiding. Although we enjoyed Cab Calloway, we always held our breaths when he came on, for fear that he might go over the edge. It's interesting: what Cab Calloway may have represented to the white community of that period—someone they could relate to. But, for the black community, Cab Calloway was not that secure an image. The point I'm trying to get to is the one I think that Barbara is making: the psychologically-destabilizing effect upon the black child of American media, and the fact that there is this absolute barrage of images that are either negative or at least non-affirming, and which—one way or another—totally exclude the reality of the black and other minorities in this country. Or, when that imagery does include these minorities, they are so misrepresented or distorted in one way or another that it may become injurious to the mental health of a young child. It is always a wonder to me that a black child survives this destabilization campaign—whether the campaign is conscious or unconscious, witting or unwitting. The fact that a black child eventually matures and becomes a taxpaying, law-abiding citizen is a phenomenon that fills me with wonder.

BARBARA BRYANT: I would like to refer to the Cab Calloway phenomenon. Whatever Cab was—whether he was the most magnificent person in the world and drew everybody and was a positive image— the truth of the matter is that, immediately behind Cab, those in control were not black. He was a black puppet on white strings. And, in the end, that is the true tragedy, the true damage. I didn't object so much to Amos n' Andy—what hurt me was that those guys on the radio could put black on their faces and make millions of dollars, while I was born with the stuff on and couldn't make a dime!

HARREL TILLMAN: That was precisely the charm of those films by Oscar Micheaux, with the Francine Everettes and the Nina Mae McKinneys in them. I don't care how black you were or how fair you were—you could see someone in those films that looked like you. If you were the "generic black," you could find somebody in there who looked like you. I could see somebody who looked like me. I could see somebody who looked like my brother. You could see those things and you could see yourself in those films that Oscar Micheaux made, but when you looked at the black that Hollywood put out, you'd see Lena Horne or Dorothy Dandridge who might not look like you. Or you'd see Bill "Bojangles" Robinson, and he might not look like you.

WILLIAM GREAVES: Those films were done at a time when there were no black images on the American screens that were in any way supportive for black people. In that context alone, they were magnificent. They revealed a wide array of characters and roles that people occupied in black society. You could see a black doctor, you could see a black lawyer, you could see a black gangster or a black whatever, and you could feel "That's right! We are people who can function in all walks of life!" In that sense, they were very valuable, useful educational tools—beyond just being sources of entertainment for black youths and black people in general.

It's true that some of these films were highly imitative and some of them were stereotypical, but by and large, the sum value and weight of these films was that they had a positive impact upon the black community. Today, when we look at these films in retrospect, they look far more archaic and some of the characters seem to be buffoons and the quality of acting seems to be somewhat low in some cases, but so were the films in the so-called "mainstream!" I think that one of the values of these films today is to show that black people can, in fact, function and create and develop a life that is a well-rounded one, and that it isn't necessary to think of black people solely as Richard Pryors and as Eddie Murphys or any of those people who are magnificent comics but who represent only one fraction of the black experience—a fraction that isn't, in ultimate terms, that significant to our survival and to our thriving in this civilization. I think that it's important that we look at these films within that context.

BARBARA BRYANT: When I was growing up, we were constantly omitted from the American media's picture of "reality." I did not know that I existed if I looked at *Life Magazine*. I did not know that I existed if I read *Time*. I did not know I existed if I read *Saturday Evening Post*.

WILLIAM GREAVES: I made a film a few years ago entitled *From These Roots*, which was on the Harlem Renaissance. We explored the possibility of using vintage motion picture film as part of the imagery. But we had to abandon the idea because, even though we had the resources of Exxon behind us, to go and search out the material, we found pitifully little. In addition to Bill Alexander's *By-Line Newsreels*, there was an organization called *All-American News*, but that didn't come out until the late forties, I believe. There was really nothing done on blacks except still photographs! So, one of the realizations which came to me as I made my film was that black people were not considered proper subject matter for filming. We were truly the Invisible Man of the times!

Working with Spencer Williams

Because the phenomenon of black-audience filmmaking examined in these pages came to an end in the early 1950s, those who actually worked on the films are difficult to find almost forty years later. It was mostly through the most fortuitous set of circumstances, largely helped by the international publicity the discovery of the "Tyler, Texas, Black Film Collection" generated, that we were able to contact those who, in the previous pages, gave us their testimony about those days and their own, personal involvement.

In the years since the restoration and re-presentation of the films, I have been able to locate several persons who worked with the person whom I now see to be the most unsung hero of that entire era—Spencer Williams—who managed, with his white associate, Al Sack, to make a total of nine feature films and thus became the "Oscar Micheaux of the 1940s."

It was from two of these people—white cinematograpaher Gordon Yoder and black actor-dancer Robert Orr (who was billed in Williams' films as July Jones)—that I was able to obtain the important reminiscences about Williams that I share with you here.

Gordon Yoder is a retired cinematographer, living in Dallas, who worked for many years as a lab assistant, assistant cameraman and then cameraman for Dallas' oldest studio, Jamieson Film Company. He helped to process the film for Williams' first feature, *The Blood of Jesus*, then was assistant cameraman on *Dirty Gertie From Harlem, U.S.A.* During those filmmaking experiences, he became well acquainted with Spencer Williams, and that relationship is vividly remembered by him today.

YODER: On *Dirty Gertie*, we did not start off with Spencer. After about a week, the fellow who started out directing, he just wasn't working out—things weren't getting done.

Then, at that time, Al Sack got Spencer in here. I remember, Spencer came into town, he took over, and things were working great.

On *Blood of Jesus*, Jack Whitman was the cameraman on that one. And sound recording was by R. E. "Dick" Byers. Byers is still alive—lives right here in Dallas. I didn't work on shooting this picture at all. I worked in the lab on this one. Maybe I went out and helped them on this one a little bit.

John Herman was cameraman on *Dirty Gertie* and I was assistant cameraman on that one. He died here about three or four years ago—lived over in Tyler. He was quite a famous guy in himself, he'd been to the South Pole with Byrd, one of Byrd's expeditions.

Were There Ever Any Black Persons
Behind the Camera Besides Spencer?

No. None. There were none working in the business here. I don't know whether the unions had a rule against it, but there just weren't any.

All the music was pre-recorded, all the singing, every bit of it. I don't know how they worked the lip-synch. I hadn't been in the business very long then. I came in in 1938 and I guess we shot this in 1940—copyrighted in 1941. I worked on it mostly in the lab. Jack was Jamieson's cameraman at that time. The crew was from Jamieson. Probably,

Al Sack contracted with Jamieson to make the film. Spencer did the editing on the picture. He came into our lab to do the editing.

It was an unusual thing to have a black person for a director, of course. It's real strange—he was the first black person I had ever worked with in my life, and had any real contact with in my life. I was real impressed with him. He was a great guy. He really was. Spencer really knew the business and he impressed me.

It's real funny—he wasn't even here in the picture for the first week. The shooting schedule must have been about three weeks, tops, so, for the first third, he wasn't even in town.

True Thompson came out and worked with the pictures. True was the one we always saw. Al Sack was the money man, but True Thompson was the one who worked out there with Spencer, and apparently was more into the distribution and knew more about it than anyone else.

He made an impression on me at the time, Spencer did, the way he could come over and get the picture out of trouble like that.

We had no problem of white guys working for a black director, none. Spencer was just like one of the bunch. As far as we (on the crew) were concerned, he was a guy who knew what he was doing, and that's all we needed to know. You know, if he hadn't known what he was doing, or something like that, you'd have gone out there and done your job anyway and just forgotten about it. But Spencer really knew his stuff. A very likeable person, very likeable, but he could take control once he got on the set. He knew how to take control. Yes, he did!

His personality was such that—well, he was a big man, and you know, it's easier for a big man to carry off something than it is for a little guy. He was a big man, and he had a commanding appearance and approach. He'd tell them what he wanted done, and that was it. He knew what he wanted done. This first director we had really didn't know what he wanted done. I forget his name, where he came from, or anything about him. All I remember about the shooting is shooting in the house, out there in South Dallas.

They came to Jamieson (Film Company in Dallas) and hired Jamieson to do it. The cameraman happened to be Jack Whitman, the sound man happened to be Dick Byers, R. E. Byers. But that's only on *The Blood of Jesus*. Jamieson had nothing to do with *Dirty Gertie*. John Herman and I were both union cameramen on *Dirty Gertie* and

Robert Orr (July Jones) as he appeared in The Girl in Room 20.

we also had stagehands. We had a union crew—it wasn't a full union crew, like you'd have on a regular picture, but we had a cameraman and assistant that were union, and the stage hands.

Spencer got what he wanted pretty damn quick, without a lot of takes. This other guy, the first director we had—he was helpless. That's what got True upset. And, of course, when True got upset, Al Sack got upset, because it was Al's money. But Spencer had no more problems, and finished up fine.

Later, I'd see Spencer on "Amos n' Andy." He was just great. I thought he was just perfect in that thing.

Robert Orr (screen name July Jones) is also retired now, and lives in Houston. He worked with Spencer Williams in 1946 and 1947. In *Dirty Gertie*, he and his dance team partner, Howard Galloway, played bit parts and did a specialty tap dance. He then played the male lead in *The Girl In Room 20* as well as in *Beale Street Mama*. Finally, he was 'second banana' to Williams in the cast of *Juke Joint*, Williams' last film.

ORR: Spencer Williams came to San Antonio, looking for talent. He had heard of my dancing partner and myself. So, he came by my high school and spoke to Mrs. Hemmings, who was my English teacher. She said, "If anybody can do it, Orr can do it, because he's got pretty good talent."

So, he said, "Well, I'll find out what kind of talent he's got after I see him work."

So, me and Galloway, my dancing partner, danced for him.

He said, "Well, I want you to act in the movie, but you have to be a star, a leading man."

So, True Thompson, who wrote the script for the film, it was called *Beale Street Mama*, told me I was to be a street sweeper in the movie. I'm sweeping down the street, and I find a big hunk of money. And then, Spence, he comes to me and he says, "Whooee! What you gonna do with all that money?"

I say, "I don't know."

He says, "Well, sir, we're going down the line, and we'll see what we can do with this money."

We go to a night club, rich men. We're all sharp in tuxedos, tails and all. And I'm supposed to be a big shot, so he tells me, "We're gonna name you July Jones."

The only thing I resent about that is this—it's all right, but they should have had my name and *then* "July Jones." Then everybody would know, see?

After they saw me on the screen, everybody said, "Well, that's July Jones." Boys in the army—that was during the war, see—told me about they had a furlough and went to the movie in Philadelphia, and who did they see? They came back and said, "You're July Jones! We saw you way up the country!" So, the name stuck.

Then, Sack came back after we made *Beale Street Mama*, and then that's when we went to Dallas to make *Juke Joint*. Part of it started in San Antonio, then we went up in South Dallas to shoot the middle, then back to San Antonio to finish it.

You know the theater in *Juke Joint* where the beauty contest is? That was called "Don's Keyhole," it was a club in San Antonio. When we were making *Juke Joint* up in Dallas, we thought we were gonna have a problem. We didn't have a location at first. But it came out just fine.

We found a little club—a real club—and everything was just fine. That big club in Dallas was the Rose Room, down on Thomas. Then, after we shot the film, my partner and I had a dancing engagement there, for three weeks. So, everything went fine.

The Girl in Room 20 was also made in San Antonio.

Then, we made *Dirty Gertie From Harlem, U.S.A.* Now, part of that was made in Fort Worth, and part was made in Dallas. Another part of it was made in San Antonio. In *Dirty Gertie*, there was a role that called for an old woman fortune-teller, and they couldn't find anybody just right. So, Spencer said, "Give me a thousand dollars, and I'll do it." Spencer found a great big old dress and he put that bandanna around his head, and he was something else!

At that time, actors weren't paid too much. For playing the lead in *Beale Street Mama*, they paid me eight hundred dollars.

Now, we had a picture called *Go Down, Death!*, then *Of One Blood*. In one of them, I just did a jitterbug act with one of the girls. My big dramatic roles were in *The Girl in Room 20*, *Beale Street Mama*, *Dirty Gertie* and *Juke Joint*.

Working with Spencer was just fine—it was funny! He'd keep you laughing the whole time you were working with him.

The relationship between blacks and whites working on those films was good. We didn't have but three white men. Everybody got along fine, no problem. Everybody always got paid, not like some of those films you hear about.

Spencer would always give me a whole script to start with, already written out. While he was directing, he'd say, "Take the script and read it. Now, when you're ready, let me know."

I'd read the script and tell him I was ready, and he'd say, "O.K., Orr, this is what you do, Orr." He'd go through the motions himself, then he'd say, "You ready?"

I'd say, "I'm ready."

He'd say, "Roll it!"

I'd go through with it, then I'd say, "How'd I do?" He'd say, "You did fine," and we'd go on like that.

There weren't many re-takes. We did a re-take on something, but it didn't take long. Most of the times, we'd get it in one take. The guy that was the sponsor was saving money, you know what I mean?

So, everything went fine, and we didn't have any problems.

The last time I saw Spencer was when he came down and said he had a big opportunity up in New York, and that I may be able to get in on it, too. He brought a script with him. It was from the "Amos n' Andy" show. He had me read some of it, and thought I could get the part. I was supposed to go up to New York to read for the people up there, but my wife told me she wouldn't want to live in New York if I did get the job—she was expecting then, you see. So, that was that. I hated it, because, at that time, that was one of my 'big breaks.'

A Final Comment
"We Could Have Been Friends"

I spent most of my childhood—which took place during the 1930s and early 1940s—in eastern Texas. My home town was Longview, population approximately 75,000 in those years.

As I looked back, in later decades, upon that place, it often seemed like a paradise to me—wide-open pastures, creeks and copses of sweet-gum and pine that were my solitary playgrounds, and days then were very, very long. But, as in most stories of paradise, there were snakes, not only the literal ones—cottonmouth moccasins and the occasional rattler—but the figurative snakes of poverty and ethnic prejudice.

Those years were, of course, during the Great Depression. I can remember how we celebrated when my father's monthly salary was raised to a hundred dollars—roughly twenty-five dollars a week. My parents tried to "shelter" me from their own worries about money, but a child always knows what his parents are feeling. We "got by" and I cannot remember going hungry or ragged.

But our housekeeper, Celia Belle (who had been named after my paternal great-aunt), had to manage on the four dollars a week which my father paid her out of our twenty-five.

For many of my childhood years, I spent more time with Celia Belle than I did with my mother, especially after my mother went to work in my father's office in order to bring in a little more money each month. Celia Belle worked very hard, and for long hours. She arrived each morning to cook breakfast as the family was rising, and had supper on the table each night before she went home to her own children. Still, she took time to do a lot of extra things for me. In summers, if

I could pick a lard pail full of blackberries down in the pasture, she would always make a cobbler for me. At other times, she would make another of my favorites, banana pie. On those nights when my parents paid her a little extra to sit with me while they were out, she worked on a quilt for my bed, which had little boys with paper hats in each of its squares. When Celia Belle, a tall, angular woman who always had a smile for me, would come to work in the mornings or leave in the evenings, we would kiss. We did, that is, until my mother told me that I shouldn't kiss her any more.

"Why?" I wanted to know.

"Because black people are different from us," she said, carefully.

"Yes, I know," I replied. "Their skin is darker. But why does that mean I shouldn't kiss her?"

"Well, they don't make as much money as we do, and they can't always afford doctors to keep them well, like we can. So they sometimes have—diseases—that you can catch with a kiss."

"Oh."

Celia Belle certainly didn't look "diseased" to me, and she seemed as strong as my father in the things she could lift and carry, but that "reasoning," plus the parental commandment, brought an end to our kisses. Not kissing Celia Belle was a source of great discomfort to me for awhile thereafter; perhaps it was for her, too. But a wedge had been driven between us which wasn't there before.

Still, I mourned for a long time when, during the war, she moved to California to work in a bomber plant. There, she had heard, black folk were paid the same wages as white folk for doing the same work. In the years that followed, I still thought of her a lot, and missed her. When I was married, almost fifteen years later, she somehow found out about it and sent what must have been one of our most expensive gifts, a three-tiered ceramic candle-holder with angels. After this reconnection, we corresponded for a while, then lost track of each other again. Today, I do not know whether she is alive or dead, but I hope that she lives.

Frail and faulty though our relationship was, I count myself deeply fortunate to have had my friendship with Celia Belle, which turned out to be the only personal relationship I was to have with a member of another ethnic group in my formative years.

It was not that I did not want other relationships. When, at the movies, my favorite *Our Gang* series would come onto the screen, I always enjoyed Spanky and Alfalfa and Froggy, and laughed at their antics. I was fascinated, though, with Stymie, the only black member of the gang. Somehow, the others seemed like unreal "child actors" to me, figments of our corporate imagination, but I would have liked to have had Stymie for a friend.

When we left Longview and moved to the comparative metropolis of Waco, Texas, during the war years so that my father, too, could work at one of the defense plants where the money was good, I made friends with a black fellow my own age who was working at an ice cream shop not far from our rented apartment. When I enticed him to come home with me, he was very nervous, very quiet. Although she was polite to him, my mother told me, when he had gone, that such friendships "just don't work out." Again, I heard that we were "different," and that those differences meant that we should keep a respectful distance from each other.

I was not to have my next black friend for more than two decades.

As I have looked back, in my later years, upon those early experiences, my usual feeling about them has been a mixture of sorrow, loss, and anger. I believe that my childhood—and thus, my adult life—would have been so much richer if I had experienced genuine friendships across ethnic lines. I deeply regret, still, the inhibition which grew between myself and Celia Belle, who was really a second mother to me in all those years. But how can I be angry with my mother, who is now gone, for trying, patiently and carefully, to give me the "wisdom" which she had inherited from her elders, and fully believed? I can hardly imagine how a person of her generation could have grown up in East Texas (or, for that matter, almost anywhere else in the English-speaking world) without having some ethnic prejudice drummed into them along with their mother's milk. No, perhaps "drummed into" is the wrong concept. "Slipped to them" would be more like the reality in many cases, all the more insidious because it was so subtle and genteel.

The Victims of Prejudice

Although we usually think of minorities as being the only victims of prejudice, I believe that majorities are no less its victims. The price majorities pay for their victimization may be less onerous in the moment, but it is no less damaging in the long run.

I cannot say with any authority how prejudice "worked" in any other communities or families, but I can describe its inner workings within my own community and family. Prejudice requires ignorance—either the ignorance of accident or the ignorance born of an unwillingness to observe. I maintain that the prejudice against black people by the white people in my early experience was due to the fact that we were ignorant of black people except as laborers, as servants. We "knew" them only upon that basis, and saw only the facet of their lives which was revealed in those activities. We had no experiential knowledge of them as members of families, as practitioners of religion, as people involved in their community's processes. More importantly, we did not know their hopes, their fears, their desires, and their dreams. To avoid or dispel prejudice, we must enter another's mind and heart.

The Mask

Part of our majority ignorance was caused by our unwillingness to know black people in any way other than the ways our elders had known them. Another part of our ignorance was maintained, however, by black people's unwillingness to be known, intimately and realistically. They wore "the mask" when they were around us. This is not to say that black people consciously and intentionally aided our prejudice by withholding their reality. As I understand "the mask," it was a very necessary protective shield which their ethnic forebears learned to wear very quickly after they reached these shores. Through the generations, it was still a necessary shield, to be taught to their children as soon as they could learn it. It was born, and survived, out of fear that whites would be even harsher if they knew what a black person was really thinking, what they really said when no whites were around to hear, or what their private lives were really like. It was not all fear, of course. There was a lot of anger and innate nobility behind the mask, too. You do not give another person, or group of people, insight into your personal reality if you think they will not respect and value that insight. Why should you? Let them go on in their ignorance. You can laugh, even, at their ignorance. They will think you are laughing at their unfunny jokes.

As a child, I would sometimes wander into "their section of town" in search of a drug store which had a selection of comic books I had not already gone through. I would be nervously aware that the presence of even a small white person had a way of stopping lively conversations and bringing an apparent pall onto the street corner or inside the store, which seemed to lift when I headed away.

Movies from Behind the Mask

We had three movie theaters in the town of my childhood. The Arlene was the "new" one, and it gave me my first experience of genuine air conditioning. I did not get to go there very often because it was more expensive than the other two theaters and there was also a parental suspicion that cold air in the middle of the summer might be one of the causes of the dread new disease, infantile paralysis.

Then, there was the Rita, a much smaller theater, and—finally—the Rembert. The Rembert was old and had a musty smell compounded of dusty curtains, stale popcorn oil and the dirty tennis shoes of generations of kids. The Rembert was the only theater which had a balcony, and this was where the black people of our town came to watch the movies. Sooner or later—the Rembert was a second- or third-run house—they saw all the same movies the white folk saw. Although I cannot remember ever hearing them laughing or cheering or shouting at the screen like we boys did down below, I knew they were there, because I could occasionally hear them, before the show started, moving around the backless benches they had to sit on while we sat in the comparative comfort of wooden, bolted-to-the-floor rows of folding seats which curved to fit the body.

On rare occasions, black people would also come to see movies at the Rita. This was only on "Juneteenth," the anniversary of the date when the Emancipation Proclamation finally took effect in Texas. Or, when the theater manager decided to throw a "Midnight Jamboree." I think that the beginning of the concept of "midnight movies" was with this kind of event, when a (usually white) theater owner decided he could make some extra money from an entirely black audience by choosing a time when no white patron would be interested in coming to the theater, and then programming one of "their" movies, maybe two.

I can remember coming out of the Rita Theatre with my parents, it must have been very late one night, and seeing a wonderful sign on the sidewalk. It screamed "Midnight Jamboree—Tonight!!" and—in red and black—beautiful women danced, dressed only in banners. I was immediately interested, not only in scantily-clad red-and-black ladies but even more in staying up later than I had ever done before.

"Why don't we go see that?" I asked.

"Sssssssh!" was my parents' embarrassed warning.

"What's wrong?" I whispered back, blushing for having broken some rule and wanting to know which one it was.

"It's only for black people. It's one of those black movies."

Although I knew I was not to be allowed to see it—not just by my parents but by the theater people, and maybe even by the black people themselves—I was, nevertheless, even more fascinated with the prospect.

"What could they be like?" I wondered. I had seen Stymie in the *Our Gang* series up on the screen. I had seen Stepin Fetchit and Bill "Bojangles" Robinson, too, in some of the Shirley Temple movies. I genuinely enjoyed Fetchit and Robinson, but Shirley tried to act so grown-up and cute that she embarrassed me. I always shrank down into my seat, my face burning with shame, when I saw her up there. Maybe I was worried that she would make everyone in the theater think that all kids her age, including me, were that way. It took a lapse of many precious years before I was to realize that this could be precisely how many black people felt when they saw themselves represented upon the screen only by buffoons and servants, even while they were glad to see at least some representation of their group.

But what could those "black movies" be like? I really wanted to know.

That must have been around 1939. I was not to find out what those movies were like until almost half a century later.

How the Films Might Have Made a Difference

I am no believer in the mystical power of any amount of film or tele-vison to convert viewers from law-abiding to law-breaking, from angels to devils, or—more importantly in this context—vice-versa. The years I have spent personally critiquing and collating almost fifty years worth of research in the matter (as a member of the Effects Research Panel of the President's Commission on Obscenity and Pornography from 1969–1971, as well as in the process of doing my dissertation on film, television and their relationship to anti-social behavior) have thoroughly convinced me that there is no direct causal effect of these arts/media upon attitudes, values and behaviors about which society is deeply concerned. This is too bad, of course, not only for those who would like to find a simple and censorable cause for society's ills, but also for those who would like to find a simple and manipulable "fix" for those ills.

This is not to say, however, that cinema (as well as television) can-not be effective educational tools. In fact, another body of research proves that they can be, and that they can teach even things we would rather they did not. Given a person who is already committed to a life of crime, a television show in which a burglar uses a plastic credit card to enter a hotel room may show him a more excellent way to do his dirty deeds. Moving images upon the screen, any amount of them, cannot turn that person from law-abiding citizen to burglar, but they can teach him how to be a better burglar. Conversely, a documentary which dramatically depicts the plight of a people starving in a foreign land may help a person who is already a benefactor to such causes to direct his funds toward that country's relief program rather than another's. But any amount of such films would not have the strength to turn a constitutionally selfish person into a liberal benefactor. Moving images alone cannot convert people.

What cinema (and its questionable child, television) can do, how-ever, is to influence loosely-held attitudes upon subjects for which the viewer has little or no prior experiential knowledge. In other words, any amount of moving images upon a screen cannot do effective battle with even a small amount of direct experience; but where that experi-ence is lacking, and there is no prior, deeply-held reason for clinging to misinformation, moving images can sometimes win by default. For instance, if one knows nothing of the marriage rituals of Sherpas and finally sees a film which purports to depict those practices, and depicts them with apparent sincerity and faithfulness, one is likely to believe what is thus presented, and to keep on believing—with whatever subtle attitudinal and behavioral changes in the believer which may be consequent—until the film's information is challenged by some stronger source, such as a better film, report from a friend who has been to a Sherpa wedding, or direct experience.

Thus, there is a small opening left through which film might better our attitudes—and perhaps our behavior—towards another group of people about whom we have little or no information.

For instance, let us hypothesize that a parent has based her precaution about interaction with members of another ethnic group upon her information that "they are not like us; if they were more like us, it would be all right." This attitudinal set may abide as long as the parent has no information to counter those assumptions, but what if she (or he) sees some films depicting the previously-unknown family, religious, and social life of the other group, presented from a source and in a manner which seems sincere and authoritative? If the attitudinal set is not simply a cloak for a more deeply-held prejudice (such as fear that recognition of another group might threaten our own group's shaky hold on certain kinds of jobs), and is genuinely and naïvely founded on misinformation, then getting new information which seems to be true may change that attitudinal set.

The pity about the Rembert and Rita Theatres of my childhood (and all those other thousands of movie theaters across America they represented) was that, although the black people up in the balconies were seeing white films, white people were not seeing the films which were written, directed and produced by black artists. In the Hollywood films, black folk were seeing depictions of white family life, white political life, white courtship and romance, and the better films showed something genuine about the hopes, fears, and dreams of the majority population. In the films which were being made for black audiences at the time, the same qualities and aspects of black life could have been seen by whites, but—except for projectionists and an occasional theater owner, whites were not looking. If we had done a turnabout, and had whites in the balconies when the black films were being shown, I do not believe that white ethnic prejudice about blacks could have flourished quite as luxuriantly as it did in the 1930s and 1940s. White kids—and their parents—would have had too much information about the realities of black lifestyle. As it was, whites were seeing some depictions of black family, religious and social life, but these images were Hollywood-made and, in most cases, only served to support white prejudice that blacks were, at best, funny, entertaining, and exotic.

Prejudice has always been built on a foundation of ignorance. One of the definitions for the term in *Webster's Third New International Dictionary* (G. C. Merriam Co., Springfield, Mass., 1976) is "an opinion or leaning adverse to anything without just grounds or before sufficient knowledge."

Where I grew up, white people were largely ignorant of black life, so they could imagine all sorts of "differences" which seemed to require segregation. If the white majority could have been seeing these films back in the 1930s and 1940s, however, it might have been very difficult for them to avoid seeing—presented too simply and sincerely to call it pretense—the common life which we all share, always have shared and always will share. I do not see how anyone from any other ethnic group could have seen those films and not admitted, "We are far more alike than we are different."

Prejudice might have found a way around this. But then, maybe not. At least to some greater degree than we were, perhaps we could have been friends.

APPENDIX ONE

Independent Black Films: 1910–1957

The following is meant to be a listing—as complete as possible with present scholarship—of all black-cast films meant primarily for black audiences, not produced by any of the Hollywood or New York studios, and produced instead by the small independent filmmakers.

Most films in this more than half-century span, although meant primarily for black audiences, were made by white companies with white screenwriters, producers, directors, and technicians. In the following listing, however, titles of the films which were made by black companies, or which had either a black screenwriter, producer, or director are printed in **boldface** type. The name of the black company or behind-the-camera black artist is also in boldface. In the case of companies which were owned and managed by both white and black persons, this listing labels a company as "black" so long as it had at least one significant officer who was black. (In the case of such companies as Dunbar or Million Dollar Productions, the companies' designations changed as a black partner either joined or left the companies.) For primary research in company histories, this author acknowledges his debt to Henry T. Sampson's *Blacks in Black and White*, Appendix B (Scarecrow Press, 1977). Except for those films notated "short," "documentary," or "newsreel," all titles are feature-length.

When an asterisk (*) follows a citation, it indicates that a copy of the film—either on 35mm or 16mm film or on some form of videotape—exists in the Southwest Film/Video Archives.

Absent. With Clarence Brooks and George Reed. **Rosebud Film Corporation**, 1928.
Am I Guilty?. With Ralph Cooper, Sybil Lewis, "Pigmeat" Markham. Supreme Pictures, 1940.
Are Working Girls Safe?. With Ebony Players. Ebony Film Corporation, 1918 (short).

OSCAR MICHEAUX Presents "THE BETRAYAL"
Distributed by ASTOR PICTURES CORP.

As the World Rolls On. With Jack Johnson and Blanche Thompson.
Andlauer Production Company, 1921.

Bargain with Bullets. With Ralph Cooper, Lawrence Criner,
Clarence Brooks. **Story/screenplay by Ralph Cooper. Million
Dollar Productions**, 1937.

Basin Street Review. With Lionel Hampton, Sarah Vaughan, Mantan
Moreland. Studio Films, Inc., 1955.*

Beale Street Mama. With July Jones, Spencer Williams, Rosalie
Larrimore. **Directed by Spencer Williams**. Hollywood
Pictures, 1946.

Betrayal, The. With Leroy Collins, Lou Vernon, Verlie Cowan.
Written, produced and directed by Oscar Micheaux. Astor
Pictures Corporation, 1948.

Beware. With Louis Jordan, Frank Wilson, Valerie Black. Astor
Pictures Corporation, 1946.*

Big Timers. With Moms Mabley, Stepin Fetchit, Francine Everett.
All-American News & Astor Pictures Corp., 1945. (short)*

Bip Bam Boogie. With Lena Horne, Ebony Trio, Alex Brown. Company unknown, 194? (short).

Birth Mark. Cast unknown. **Produced by William Foster. Foster Photoplay Company,** 191? (short).

Birthright. With J. Homer Tutt, Evelyn Preer, Lawrence Chenault. **Written, produced and directed by Oscar Micheaux. Micheaux Film Corporation**, 1924.

Birthright (sound remake). With Ethel Moses and Alec Lovejoy. **Written, produced and directed by Oscar Micheaux. Micheaux Film Corporation**, 1939.

Black and Tan Mixup, A. With the Ebony Players. **Ebony Film Corporation,** 1918 (short).

Black Boomerang, The. No cast information. William H. Clifford Photoplay Company, 1924.

Black Cat Tales. With Buck and Bubbles (Ford Lee Washington and John Sublette). **Produced by William Foster. Foster Photoplay Company**, 1933 (short).

Black Gold. With Lawrence Criner and Kathryn Boyd. Norman Film Manufacturing Company, 1928.

Black King. With A. B. Comathiers and Vivianne Baker. Southland Pictures, 1932.*

Black Magic. No cast information. **Written, produced and directed by Oscar Micheaux. Micheaux Film Corporation**, 1932.

Black Sherlock Holmes. No cast information. Ebony Pictures, 1917 (short).

Black Thunderbolt. With Jack Johnson. A. A. Millman Company, 1922.

Blood of Jesus, The. With Spencer Williams and Cathryn Caviness. **Written and directed by Spencer Williams**. Sack Amusement Enterprises, 1941.*

Boarding House Blues. With "Moms" Mabley, Dusty Fletcher, Lucky Millender and his band. All-America News, Inc., 1948.*

Bob Howard's House Party. (See *Howard's House Party*.)

Body and Soul. With Paul Robeson, Julia Russell, Mercedes Gilbert. **Written, produced and directed by Oscar Micheaux. Micheaux Film Corporation**, 1924.

Boogie Woogie Blues. With Hadda Brooks. All-American News, 1948 (short).*

TODDY PICTURES COMPANY *Presents* LENA HORNE *as* The BRONZE VENUS STAR SENSATION OF "CABIN IN THE SKY" and "STORMY WEATHER" ("THE DUKE IS TOPS")

Boogie Woogie Dream. With Lena Horne, Albert Ammons, Pete
   Johnson. **Hollywood Productions**, 1942 (short).*
Boy! What A Girl!. With Duke Williams, Tim Moore, Sheila Guyse.
   Herald Pictures, 1946.
Brand of Cain, The. (See *Murder in Harlem*.)*
Broken Earth. With Clarence Muse, Freida Shaw Choir. Continental
   Pictures, 1939 (short).*
Broken Strings. With Clarence Muse and Sybil Lewis. **Screenplay by
   Clarence Muse**, Bernard Ray and David Arlen. International
   Roadshows, 1940.*
Broken Violin. With Gertrude Snelson, J. Homer Tutt, Daisy Foster.
   **Written, produced and directed by Oscar Micheaux. Micheaux
   Film Company**, 1926.
Bronze Buckeroo. With Herbert Jeffrey, Lucius Brooks, Clarence
   Brooks. **Hollywood Productions**, 1938.*
Bronze Venus. (See *The Duke is Tops*.)*
Brother. Cast unknown. **Produced by William Foster. Foster
   Photoplay Company**, 1918.

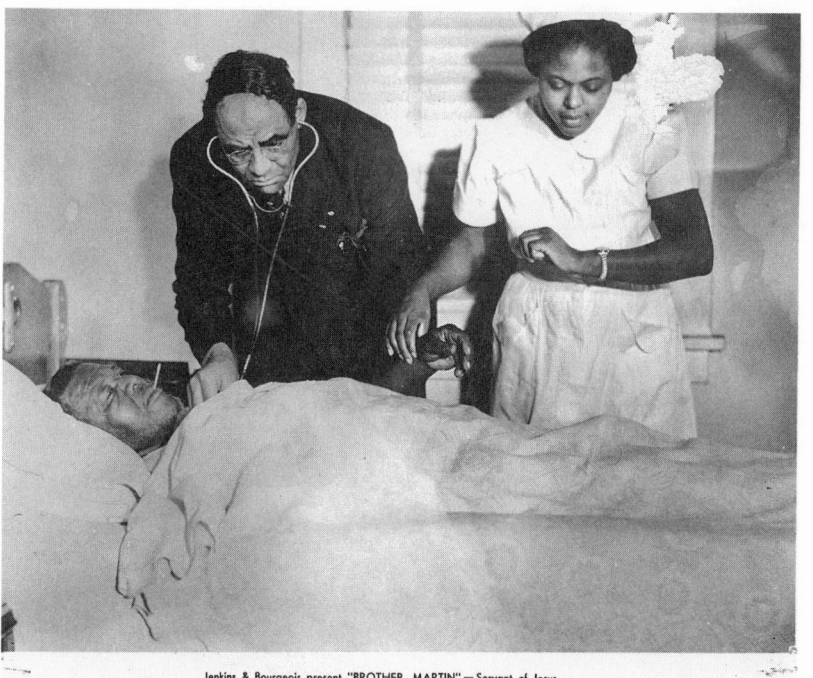

Jenkins & Bourgeois present "BROTHER MARTIN" — Servant of Jesus

Brother Martin, Servant of Jesus. With Spencer Williams. **Written and directed by Spencer Williams**. Jenkins and Bourgeois Productions, 1942.

Brute, The. With Sam Langford, Evelyn Preer, Lawrence Chenault. **Written, directed and produced by Oscar Micheaux. Micheaux Film Corporation**, 1920.

Buck and Bubbles Laugh Jamboree. With Buck and Bubbles. Ted Toddy Pictures, 1945.

Bull Dogger, The. With Bill Pickett and Anita Bush. Norman Film Manufacturing Company, 1923.

Burden of Race, The. With Edna Morton and Lawrence Chenault. Reol Productions, 1921.

Burlesque in Harlem. With Dewey "Pigmeat" Markham, George Wilshire, Vivian Harris. T. N. T. Pictures Corp, 1955.

Busted Romance, A. With the Ebony Players. Ebony Film Corporation, 1918 (short).

Butler, The. Cast unknown. **Produced by William Foster. Foster Photoplay Company**, 191? (short).

"CHILDREN OF CIRCUMSTANCE" The Most Human Story Ever Told

By-Line Newsreels. Newsreels produced by William Alexander
and Biddy Woods. **Alexander Productions,** 1953–1956.*

By Right of Birth. With Clarence Brooks and Anita Thompson.
**Screenplay by George P. Johnson. Lincoln Motion Picture
Company,** 1921 (short).

Caldonia. With Louis Jordan and Roxie Joynes. **Produced by Louis
Jordan.** Astor Pictures, 1945 (short).

Call of Duty, The. **Documentary produced by William Alexander.
Alexander Productions,** 1946.

Call of His People, The. With C. Edward Brown, Percy Verwayen and
Edna Morton. **Story by Aubrey Bowser.** Reol Motion Picture
Corporation, 1922.

Cavalcade of Harlem. No cast information. **Harlem
Productions,** 1937.

Chicago After Dark. With Lollypop Jones and Allen McMillen. All
American News, Inc., 1946 (short).

A Child in Pawn. No cast information. **D. W. D. Film
Corporation,** 1921.

Children of Circumstance. With Catherine Alexander and Ollington E. Smith. Gramercy Pictures, 1937.

Children of Fate. With Lawrence Chenault, Shingzie Howard, William Clayton. Colored Players Film Corporation, 1929.

Clef Club Five Minutes for Train. No cast information. **Colored and Indian Film Company**, 191? (short).

***Colored America on Parade*. Newsreel produced by Edward W. Lewis**, 1940.

Colored American Winning His Suit, The. No cast information, other than "citizens of Jersey City, N. J., and vicinity." **Frederick Douglas Film Company**, 1916 (short).

Colored Americans. Newsreel. Mutual Film Corporation, 1918.

Colored Americans in the Nation's Capital. Newsreel. Ted Toddy Corporation, 194?.

Colored Champions of Sport. Newsreel, including John Borican and Gil Cruter. **Produced by Edward W. Lewis**, 1940.

Colored Championship Baseball Game, The. Newsreel?. **Foster Photoplay Company**, 191?.

Colored Men in White. Documentary. Ted Toddy Pictures, 194?.

Colored Troops at Chillicothe. Newsreel. Finley Film Company, no date.

Come Back. With Louise Fullen and K. D. Nollan. **Produced by Leigh Whipper**. Enterprise Film Company, 1922.

Come On, Cowboy. With Mantan Moreland and Mauryne Brent. Goldmax Productions, 1948.

Comes Midnight. With Eddie Green, James Baskett, Amanda Rudolph. **Produced by Eddie Green. Sepia Art Productions**, 1940 (short).

Condemned Men. (See ***Four Shall Die***.)

The Conjure Woman. With Evelyn Preer and Percy Verwayten. **Written, Produced and Directed by Oscar Micheaux. Micheaux Film Corporation**, 1926.

The Corpse Accuses. No cast information. Toddy Pictures, 1946.

Cow-Cow Boogie. With Dorothy Dandridge, West Gale, Troy Brown. **Produced by Fritz Pollard, Soundies Distributing**, 1942.

Crime Street. No cast information. Toddy Pictures, 194?.

Crimson Fog, The. With Thomas Moseley, Inez Clough, Lawrence Chenault. **Paragon Pictures**, 1932.

Goldmax Productions **"COME ON, COWBOY!"** Mantan Moreland
Toddy Pictures Company Mauryne Brent, all colored cast

Crimson Skull, The. With Anita Bush, Lawrence Chenault, Bill
Pickett. Norman Film Company, 1921.

Crooked Money. (See ***While Thousands Cheer***.)

Custard Nine. No cast information. **Assistant Producer Clarence
Muse**. Harris Dixon Film Company, 1911 (short).

Dark and Cloudy. With Lillian Biron and George Ovey. Gaiety
Comedies, 1919 (short).

Dark Manhattan. With Ralph Cooper, Cleo Herndon, Clarence
Brooks. **Production and Story by George Randol, Directed by
Ralph Cooper** and Harry Fraser. **Cooper-Randol
Productions**, 1937.

Darktown Affair. No cast information. Mt. Olympus Distributing
Company, 1921 (short).

Darktown Revue. No cast information. **Written, Produced, and
Directed by Oscar Micheaux. Micheaux Film Corporation**, 1931.

Darktown Strutters' Ball. No cast information. **Directed by George
Randol**. No releasing company, no date.

Daughter of Pharoah, A. No cast information. Trinity Film
Corporation, 1920.

Daughter of the Congo. With Kathleen Noisette, Lorenzo Tucker, Clarence Reed. **Written, Directed and Produced by Oscar Micheaux. Micheaux Film Corporation**, 1930.

Daughters of the Isle of Jamaica. Documentary. Lenwall Productions, 1937.*

Day in the Magic City of Birmingham, A. Newsreel. Pyramid Picture Corporation, 1920.

Day in the Nation's Capital, A. Newsreel. Monumental Pictures Corporation, 191?.

Debtor to the Law. No cast information. Norman Film Manufacturing Company, 1924.

Deceit. With Ida Anderson, Evelyn Preer, Cleo Desmond. **Written, Produced and Directed by Oscar Micheaux. Micheaux Film Corporation**, 1921.

Devils, The. No cast information. E & H Distributing Company, 1923 (short).

Devil's Daughter, The. With Nina Mae McKinney and Hamtree Harrington. Goldberg Productions, 1939.*

Devil's Disciple, The. With Evelyn Preer and Lawrence Chenault. **Written, Produced and Directed by Oscar Micheaux. Micheaux Film Corporation**, 1926.

Devil's Match, The. With Walter Long and Bobbie Smart. North State Film Company, 1923 (short).

Dirty Gertie From Harlem, U.S.A. With Francine Everette, Don Wilson, July Jones. **Directed by Spencer Williams.** Sack Amusement Enterprises, 1946.*

Disappearance of Mary Jane, The. With Chicago Bathing Girls, and Jimmie Cox. Acme Film Distribution Company, 1921 (short).

Dixie Love. With Lucille Poe and Richard Gregg. **Paragon Pictures**, 1933.

Do the Dead Talk? With the Ebony Players. Ebony Film Corporation, 1918 (short).

Doing Their Bit. Documentary. **Toussaint Motion Picture Company**, 1918.

Double Deal. With Jeni LeGon, Monte Hawley, Maceo Sheffield. **Screenplay by Flournoy E. Miller**. International Road Shows, 1939.*

Dreamer, The. With Mantan Moreland, June Richmond, Mabel Lee. Astor Pictures, 1948.

Dress Rehearsal. With Eddie Green. **Sepia Art Picture Company**, 1939 (short).

Drums O' Voodoo. (See *Voodoo Drums.*)

Duke Is Tops, The. With Ralph Cooper, Lena Horne, Lawrence Criner. **Million Dollar Pictures**, 1938.*

Dusky Virgin, The. No cast information. **Paragon Pictures**, 1932.

Easy Money. With S. H. Dudley, Edna Morton, Evelyn Ellis. Reol Productions, 1921.

Easy Street. With Richard B. Harrison and Lorenzo Tucker. **Written, Produced and Directed by Oscar Micheaux. Micheaux Film Corporation**, 1930.

Ebony Parade. With Cab Calloway, Count Basie, Mantan Moreland. Astor Pictures, 1947 (short).

Eddie Green's Laugh Jamboree. With Eddie Green and Ernestine Jones. A compilation of *Comes Midnight*, *Dress Rehearsal*, and *What Goes Up*. All originally produced by **Sepia Arts Company**, distributed in this format by Toddy Pictures, Inc., 1947.

Eleven P. M.. With Marion R. Williams, Sammie Fields, Richard Maurice. **Written, Produced and Directed by Richard Maurice. Maurice Productions**, 1928.

Exile, The. With Eunice Brooks, Charles Moore, Charles Randol. **Written, Produced and Directed by Oscar Micheaux. Micheaux Film Corporation**, 1931.

Eyes of Youth. With Abbie Mitchell. Quality Amusement Company, 1920.

Fall Guy. No cast information. **Produced by William Foster. Foster Photoplay Company**, 1913 (short).

Fight Never Ends, The. With Joe Louis, Ruby Dee, William Greaves, Harrel Tillman. **Produced by William Alexander. Alexander Productions**, 1947.

Fight That Ghost. With Pigmeat Markham, John Murray, Sidney Easton. Toddy Pictures, 1946.

Fighting Americans. Newsreel. Toddy Pictures, 1943.

Fighting Deacon, The. With Tiger Flowers and Walt Miller. Milton Star Distributors, 1926.

Flames of Wrath, The. With Roxie Mankins, John Burton, Charles Pearson. **Western Film Productions**, 1923.

Flaming Crisis, The. With Dorothy Dunbar and Calvin Nicholson. **Monarch Productions**, 1924.

Flamingo. With Herbert Jeffrey and Dorothy Dandridge. Stillman Pond Productions, 1947 (short).

Flicker Up. With Billy Eckstine and May Lou Harris. **Alexander Productions**, 1946 (short).

Flying Ace, The. With Kathryn Boyd, Larence Criner, B. DeLegge. Norman Film Manufacturing Company, 1926.

Fool and Fire. No cast information. **Foster Photoplay Company**, 1927 (short).

Foolish Lives. With Frank Chapman and Henry Harris. Young Producers' Filming Company, 1922.

Fool's Errand. With William Fontaine and Shingzie Howard. No production company. No date.

Fool's Promise, A. No cast information. White Film Corporation, 1921.

For His Mother's Sake. With Jack Johnson, Matty Wilkens, Adrian Joyce. **Blackburn Velde Productions**, 1921.

Four Shall Die. With Dorothy Dandridge and Neil Webster. **Million Dollar Productions**, 1946.

Frederick Douglass' The House on Cedar Hill. Documentary. **Produced by Carlton Moss**, 1953.

From Cotton Patch to Congress. No cast information. M. W. Baccus Film Company, 1922.

Gang Smashers. With Nina Mae McKinney, Lawrence Criner, Monte Hawley. **Screenplay by Ralph Cooper. Million Dollar Productions**, 1939.

Gang War. With Ralph Cooper, Gladys Snyder, Lawrence Criner. **Million Dollar Productions**, 1939.*

Gangsters On the Loose. (See *Bargain With Bullets*.)

George Washington Carver. With Dr. George Washington Carver and Booker T. Washington III. Bryant Productions, 1940.

Georgia Rose. With Clarence Brooks and Evelyn Preer. Aristo Films, 1930.

Ghost of Tolston's Manor, The. With Andrew Bishop and Lawrence Chenault. **Written, Produced and Directed by Oscar Micheaux**, 1934.

HARRY M. POPKIN presents
NINA MAE McKINNEY in "GANG SMASHERS"
A MILLION DOLLAR PRODUCTION

Giant of His Race, A. With Mabel Homes and Walter Holeby. North
State Film Corporation, 1921.

Girl From Chicago, The. With Carl Mahon, Starr Calloway, Grace
Smith. **Written, Produced and Directed by Oscar Micheaux.
Micheaux Film Corporation**, 1932.*

Girl in Room 20, The. With July Jones, Geraldine Brock, Spencer
Williams. **Directed by Spencer Williams**. Jenkins and Bourgeois
Productions, 1946.*

Go Down, Death!. With Myra Hemmings, Samuel James, Spencer
Williams. **Written and Directed by Spencer Williams**. Sack
Amusement Enterprises, 1944.*

God's Stepchildren. With Alice B. Russell and Ethel Moses. **Written,
Produced and Directed by Oscar Micheaux. Micheaux Film
Corporation**, 1937.*

Going to Glory, Come to Jesus. With Irene Hopper and Walter
Freeman. **Story by Wesley Wilson**. Toddy Pictures, 1947.

Golden Pearls of Progress. No cast information. Exquisite Productions,
191? (short).

ROYAL GOSPEL PRODUCTIONS   "GOING TO GLORY"—COME TO JESUS   *World Wide Release By*
Presents   ALL COLORED CAST-GOSPEL CHOIR   ROYAL GOSPEL PRODUCTIONS

Gone Harlem. With Jimmy Baskett and Ethel Moses. Creative Cinema
Corporation, 1939.

Grafter and the Maid, The. No cast information. **Screenplay by Jerry
Mills. Produced by William Foster. Foster Photoplay Company**,
1913 (short).

Greatest Sin, The. With Mae Evelyn Lewis and Victor Nix. **Trio
Productions**, 1922 (short).

Green-Eyed Monster, The. With Jack Austin and Louise Dunbar.
Norman Film Manufacturing Company, 1921.

Gun Moll (see *Gang Smashers*)

Gunsaulus Mystery, The. With Evelyn Preer, Lawrence Chenault,
Dick Abrams. **Written, Produced and Directed by Oscar
Micheaux. Micheaux Film Corporation**, 1921.

Harlem After Midnight. With Billy Eckstine and Ann Baker. No
distributor, 1947.

Harlem After Midnight. With Lorenzo Tucker and Alfred "Slick"
Chester. **Written, Produced and Directed by Oscar Micheaux.
Micheaux Film Corporation**, 1935.

ALFRED N. SACK presents **BILL ROBINSON** in **"HARLEM IS HEAVEN"**
with EUBIE BLAKE'S ORCHESTRA and NEW YORK'S FAMOUS COTTON CLUB ENTERTAINERS
Distributed by SACK AMUSEMENT ENTERPRISES

Harlem Follies. With Savannah Churchill, Sheila Guyse, John Kirby
and His Band. Herald Pictures, 1950.

Harlem Hotshots. With Cora Harris, Leon Gross and His Orchestra,
Stringbeans Jackson. **Directed by Spencer Williams?** Sack
Amusement Enterprises, 1940.*

Harlem Is Heaven. With Bill Robinson, John Mason, Putney
Dandridge. Lincoln Productions, 1932.*

Harlem on Parade. With Lena Horne. Goldberg Productions. No date.

Harlem on the Prairie. With Herb Jeffries, Mantan Moreland,
Spencer Williams. **Supervised by Maceo Sheffield**. Associated
Pictures, 1938.

Harlem Rides the Range. With Herb Jeffries, Lucius Brooks, Spencer
Williams. **Screenplay by Spencer Williams and Flournoy E.
Miller**, Hollywood Productions, 1939.*

Harlem Variety Revue. With Lionel Hampton, Herb Jeffries, Faye
Adams. Studio Films, 1955 (short).

Harlemania. With Ethel Moses, Jimmy Baskette, Count Basie.
Creative Cinema Corporation, 1938.

Harry Wills in Training. With Harry Wills. Acme Film Distributors, 1924 (short).

Hearts of the Woods. With Clifford Harris and Lawrence McGuire. Superior Arts Productions, 1921.

Hell Cats. With Dewey "Pigmeat" Markham. Toddy Pictures, 194?.

Hello, Bill. With Bill Robinson, Billy Higgins, Joe Byrd. Famous Artists Company, 1929.

Hell's Alley. With Thomas Moseley and Jean Webb. **Screenplay by Hattie Watkins and Jean Webb. Paragon Pictures**, 1931.

Heroic Black Soldiers of the War. Documentary. **Frederick Douglass Film Company**, 1919 (short).

Hi De Ho. With Cab Calloway and His Orchestra, Ida James and Jeni LeGon. All-American News, 1947 (short).*

Highest Tradition, The. Documentary. **Alexander Productions**, 1946.

His Great Chance. With Sandy Burns, Bobbie Smart, Tim Moore. North State Film Corporation, 1923.

His Harlem Wife. (See *Life Goes On*.)

Home Brew. No information on cast or company, 1920.

Homesteader, The. With Charles Lucas and Evelyn Preer. **Written, Directed and Produced by Oscar Micheaux. Micheaux Film Corporation**, 1919.

Hot Dogs. No cast information. White Film Company, 1921.

House Behind the Cedars, The. With Shingzie Howard and Lawrence Chenault. **Written, Produced and Directed by Oscar Micheaux. Micheaux Film Corporation**, 1924.

House Rent Party. With Dewey "Pigmeat" Markham and John "Rastus" Murray. Toddy Pictures, 1946.

How High Is Up? With Moss and Fry. **Seminole Film Company**, 1922 (short).

Howard-Lincoln Football Game. Newsreel. Momumental Pictures Corporation, 1921.

Howard's House Party. With Bob Howard and Noble Sissle. Century Films, 1947 (short).

Hypocrites, The. With the Ebony Players. Ebony Film Corporation, 1917 (short).

Ill Wind. No cast information. Toddy Pictures, 1946 (short).

In the Depths of Our Hearts. With Herman de la Valades and
   Augusta Williams. **Royal Garden Film Company**, 1920.

In the Shadows. No cast information. Mesco Productions, 1923.

Injustice. (See *Loyal Hearts*.)

It Happened in Harlem. With Slick and Slack and Phil Gomez.
   All-American News, 1945.*

Janitor, The. With Sam Robinson and Samuel Jacques. Ebony Film
   Corporation, 1918.

Jasper Landry's Will. With William E. Fontaine and Shingzie
   Howard. **Written, Produced and Directed by Oscar Micheaux**.
   Micheaux Film Corporation, 1923.

Jazz Festival. With Lionel Hampton, Mantan Moreland, Nipsey
   Russell. Studio Films, Inc., 1955.

Jazz Hounds. With Edna Morton. Reol Productions, 1922 (short).

Jittering Jitterbugs. With Hamtree Harrington, Lee Neuman and His
   Orchestra, Arthur White's Lindy Hoppers. No studio,
   1938 (short).

IT HAPPENED IN HARLEM
An All American Variety Production   Directed by Bud Pollard

Jivin' In Bebop. With Dizzy Gillespie and His Orchestra, Helen Humes, Ray Sneed. **Produced by William Alexander, Directed by Spencer Williams**? Sack Amusement Enterprises, 1947.*

Jivin' the Blues. With Lena Horne and Sewanee Sweethearts. No studio, 194? (short).

Joint Is Jumping, The. With John Mason, Una Mae Carlisle, Hadda Brooks. All-American News, 1948.

Juke Joint. With Spencer Williams, July Jones, Inez Newell. **Written and Directed by Spencer Williams**. Sack Amusement Enterprises, 1947.*

Junction 88. With Dewey "Pigmeat" Marhkam, Bob Howard, Noble Sissle. **Book and Lyrics by J. Augustus Smith**. Sack Amusement Enterprises, 1947 (short).*

Junior Jeeps. Cast uncredited. George Weiss Productions, 1947 (short).*

Keep Punching. With Henry Armstrong, Willie Bryant, Hamtree Harrington. **Script by J. Rosamond Johnson**. Filmart Studios, 1939.*

All American presents **"THE JOINT IS JUMPIN' "** JOHN MASON, UNA MAE CARLISLE, EDDIE SOUTH, HADDA BROOKS, PHIL MOORE FOUR, OLIVETTE MILLER, Charles Ray, Mildred Kirk, Slick and Slack, John Oscar, Frog Edwards, Bob Howard, All American Girl Band, George Lawson and his Band. Released through all American News, Inc.   Made in the U. S. A.

Killer Diller. With Dusty Fletcher, Butterfly McQueen, King Cole Trio. All-American News, 1947.*

Lady Luck. With Flournoy Miller and Mantan Moreland. Dixie National Pictures, 1940.

Law of Nature, The. With Noble Johnson and Clarence Brooks. **Lincoln Motion Picture Company**, 1917.

Lem Hawkins' Confession (See *Murder in Harlem*.)*

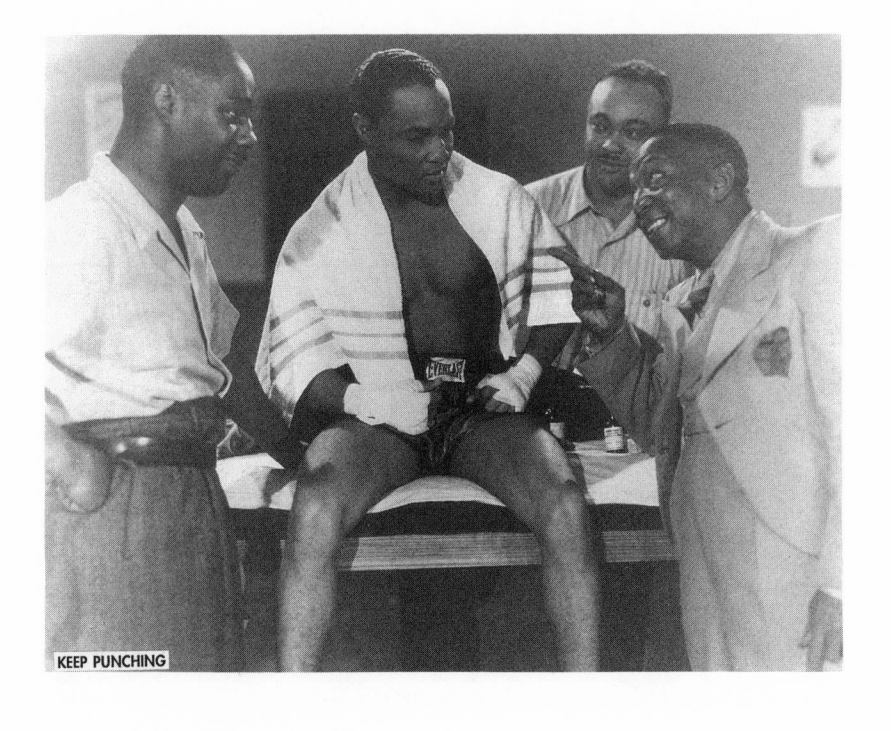

KEEP PUNCHING

Life Goes On. With Louise Beavers, Lawrence Criner, Monte Hawley. **Million Dollar Productions**, 1938.

Life in Harlem. Documentary. Sack Amusement Enterprises, 1940.

Life of Booker T. Washington, The. No cast information. Duo Art Pictures, 1940.

Life of Florence Mills, The. No cast information. Duo Art Pictures, 1940.

Life of George Washington Carver, The. No cast information. Duo Art Pictures, 1940.

Lifting As We Climb. Documentary. **Artisan Productions (National Association of Colored Women)**, 1953.

Look Out, Sister. With Louis Jordan, Suzette Harbin, Monte Hawley. Astor Pictures, 1946.*

Louisiana (See *Voodoo Drums*.)

Love and Undertakers. No cast information. **Colored and Indian Film Company**, 1918 (short).

Love Bug, The. With Billy Mills and Maud Frisbie. Norman Film Manufacturing Company, 1920 (short).

W. D. ALEXANDER presents "LOVE IN SYNCOPATION"
Distributed thru ASTOR PICTURES Corp.

Love in Syncopation. With Ruby Dee, Harrel Tillman, Powell Lindsay. **Produced by William Alexander. Alexander Productions**, 1947.

Loyal Hearts. With Sidney Preston Dones and Thais Nehli Kalana. **Directed by S. P. Dones. Democracy Film Company**, 1919.

Luck in Old Clothes. With the Ebony Players. Ebony Film Corporation, 1918 (short).

Lucky Gamblers. With Lollypop Jones and Edith Graves. All-American News, 1946.*

Lucky Ghost. With Mantan Moreland and Flournoy Miller. Dixie National Pictures, 1946.

Lure of a Woman, The. With Regina Cohee, Dr. A. Porter Davis, Charles K. Allen. **Progress Picture Association**, 1921.

Lure of the Woods. No cast or studio information, 1922.

Lying Lips. With Edna Mae Harris, Carmen Newsome, Robert Earl Jones. **Written, Produced and Directed by Oscar Micheaux. Micheaux Film Corporation**, 1939.*

LUCKY GHOST

Man from Texas, The. No cast information. **Ben-Roy Productions**, 1921.

Man's Duty, A. With Clarence Brooks. **Produced by George P. Johnson. Lincoln Motion Picture Company**, 1919.

Mantan Messes Up. With Mantan Moreland, Lena Horne, Eddie Green. **Lucky Star Productions**, 1946.

Mantan Runs for Mayor. With Mantan Moreland and Flournoy Miller. **Lucky Star Productions**, 1946.

Marching On. With Hugh Martin, George Sutton and Myra Hemmings. **Written and Directed by Spencer Williams**. Sack Enterprises, 1943.*

Marcus Garland. With Salem Tutt Whitney and Amy Birdsong. **Written, Produced and Directed by Oscar Micheaux. Micheaux Film Corporation**, 1928.

Matchless Key, The. No cast information. White Film Company, (short).

Memorial Services at the Tomb of "Prince Hall." Newsreel. **Peacock Photoplay Company**, 1922.

"Mercy" the Mummy Mumbled. With the Ebony Players. Ebony Film
Corporation, 1917 (short).

Midnight Ace, The. With A. B. Comathiere, Mabel Kelly, Susie
Sutton. **Produced by Swan Micheaux. Dunbar Film
Corporation**, 1928.

Midnight Menace. With Sybil Lewis and George Wiltshire.
All-American News, 194?.

Midnight Shadow. With Frances Redd, Buck Woods, Clinton
Rosemond. **Produced and Directed by George Randol. George
Randol Productions**, 1939.*

Milk-Fed Hero. With the Ebony Players. Ebony Film Corporation,
1918 (short).

Millionaire, The. With Grace Smith, Lawrence Criner, Lionel
Monegas. **Written, Produced and Directed by Oscar Micheaux.
Micheaux Film Corporation**, 1927.

Minister's Temptation, A. No cast information. **Democracy Film
Corporation**, 1919 (short).

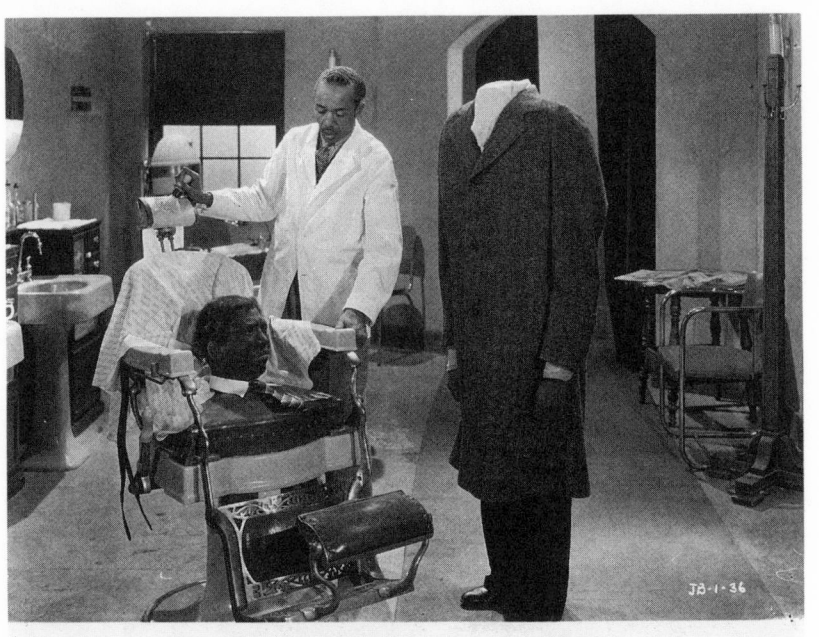

Toddy Pictures Co. presents **"MR. WASHINGTON GOES TO TOWN"** with Mantan and Miller

Miracle in Harlem. With William Greaves, Sheila Guyse, Stepin Fetchit. Herald Pictures, 1948.*

Mr. Adam's Bomb. With Eddie Green and Gene Ware. **Written and Produced by Eddie Green. Sepia Film Productions**, 1949.

Mr. Smith Goes Ghost. With Dewey "Pigmeat" Markham, Monte Hawley, Lawrence Criner. **Produced by Dewey 'Pigmeat' Markham. Screenplay by Ralph Cooper**. Toddy Pictures, 1940 (short).

Mr. Washington Goes to Town. With Mantan Moreland and Flournoy Miller. Dixie National Pictures, 1940.*

Modern Cain, A. With Norman Ward and Vivian Quarles. J. W. Fife Productions, 1921.

Moon Over Harlem. With Cora Green and Bud Harris. Meteor Productions Inc., 1939.*

Mother. No cast information. **Foster Photoplay Company**, 191? (short).

Murder in Harlem. With Clarence Brooks, Dorothy Van Engle, Bee

MURDER ON LENOX AVE. *An INTERNATIONAL ROAD SHOW Release*

Freeman. **Written, Produced and Directed by Oscar Micheaux. Micheaux Film Corporation**, 1935.*

Murder on Lenox Avenue. With Mamie Smith, Alec Lovejoy, Edna Mae Harris. **Story by Frank Wilson.** Colonnade Productions, 1941.*

Murder Rap. With Jeni LeGon, Monte Hawley and the Harlem 'Tuff' Kids. Toddy Pictures, 1942.

Murder with Music. With Bob Howard, Nellie Hill, Noble Sissle and His Orchestra. Century Productions, 1941.*

Mystery in Swing. With Monte Hawley and Marguerite Whitten. International Road Shows, 1938.*

Negro Marches On, The. Newsreel. Goldberg Productions, (no date).

Negro News Monthly. Newsreel. Monumental Pictures Corporation, (no date).

Negro News Reel. Newsreel. Will Herman Productions, 1923.

Negro of Today, The. Documentary. **C. B. Campbell Studio**, 1921.

Negro Sailor, The. With Leigh Whipper and Joel Fluellen. All-American News, 1944.